THE **A-R-T** OF PROACTIVE CRIMINAL DEFENSE

1. ARREST:

AF877991

Client is arrested by the police. What can we learn from the arrest?

2. RELEASE:

Client is released from custody . Client must understand and comply with the terms of their release or serious face consequences. Can we make things easier?

3. TRACK:

Police, prosecutor and court working together to prosecute you. How to stay informed and the opportunity to be proactive from day one.

Sarah is arrested for a DUI, now what?

Sarah reaches out to me over the weekend about a recent drunk driving arrest. It is quite common for a client to be arrested on a Thursday, Friday or Saturday night and spend a night in jail before being released. We apply the three step "A-R-T" method of review, which covers arrest, release, and tracking. For DUI's in Michigan, most defendants are released either on a personal bond or a small cash bond; the exception would if the client has an extensive criminal record, especially prior drunk driving convictions.

Along with likely release, the Defendant is given bond conditions with the most common rule being no drugs or alcohol with mandatory testing. When a potential drunk driving client reaches out, it is important to get all the paperwork in their possession; there is a lot of valuable information to be gained.

We want to be sure that there is NOT an implied consent issue, which we will get more into, and the client must understand all of their bond conditions, their ability to drive a vehicle, and when court may be. I also inquire about the status of their driver's license, past criminal history, and if they hold a CDL or a CPL. We also want to dive into their professional life, and if they hold any professional licenses or any licensing by the State.

While most clients I work with are residents of Michigan, a decent portion of DUI clients are from out of state, or at a minimum have an out of state license. It is important for a client to understand how an out of state or in-state license differ for their case, and their ability to drive.

Along with gathering this background information, it is important for a client to layout their recollection of the what happened with the police; the information is most fresh immediately after the arrest. The only issue with a DUI case is the alcohol and potential lack of memory or a false sense of what happened. Some clients remember it all, some remember parts, some nothing, and some remember, either intentionally or unintentionally the wrong thing.

After gathering background on Sarah, it turns out she is a schoolteacher in Michigan, has no prior criminal history, does not have a CDL or CPL, but tells me that she refused the breath test. This last piece of information is extremely important for an attorney to know. Sarah also sends me copies of all her paperwork, which includes a ticket, a temporary license, refusal paperwork and an inventory of her property. She also has paperwork with a TBD for her court date.

I ask Sarah to walk me through her version of the arrest as I now have access to her paperwork and can begin to piece together the evening. This will cover the ARREST portion of the A-R-T method.

Sarah tells me that she was speeding on a residential road with a speed limit of 35 MPH; she estimates she was going around 55 and was lost. She had been out with work friends celebrating the end of the school year and was trying to find her way back to the freeway; while trying to find her way, she was pulled over by the police.

Within the A-R-T approach, we also want to use three windows of inquiry. The first thing we examine in an arrest is the reason for being pulled over, stopped by the police, or how the heck did you end up interacting with a police officer, and does it meet the legal standard in Michigan.

Here we have a traffic stop by a police officer; some cases involve accidents where a police officer arrives after the "driving", a civilian may call 911, or a driver may be parked somewhere with the car not in motion. A traffic stop like Sarah is the most common. For a police officer in Michigan to make a traffic stop, the officer must have reasonable suspicion that the driver of the vehicle has committed a violation of the traffic code.

Even if in the end the driver did not, the standard is a reasonable suspicion, not probable or beyond a reasonable doubt. To challenge a traffic stop, it is an uphill battle which is helped if video is available that contradicts the officer's reason.

Here we have speeding, and if the officer reasonable believed Sarah was speeding, the traffic stop is a good stop, and would unlikely be cause for inquiry

The good news for Sarah is speeding alone is NOT a basis for impaired or intoxicated driving; sober people speed all the time, but it is a reason to be pulled over. Once on the side of the road, the officer will not interact with Sarah. Under the law, Sarah is not required to speak or perform any tests for the officer; she must comply with providing her license, registration and insurance; her name is listed on this information, and she has the option of keeping her mouth closed and handing over this information.

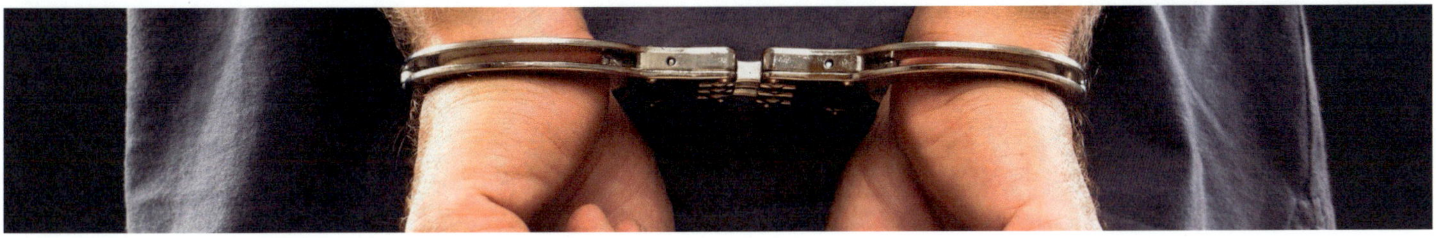

That never happens, and clients are very chatty with the officer, because that officer is trained to elicit information and make observations to assist in determining if an arrest should be made. This is now our second window of inquiry; once the stop is examined, we must now determine if the officer has probable cause to arrest the driver for a crime committed. Speeding is not a crime, so an arrest cannot be made based on that observation.

The officer will now make observations, elicit statements, and push for field sobriety tests to support the need for probable cause. It means how it sounds, is it probable that Sarah in this case committed the crime of drunk driving, which requires operation of a motor vehicle, and either impairment or intoxication. It is probable Sarah was driving as he pulled her over, there was only one person in the car, and Sarah admits to leaving a work party and getting lost.

The probability of driving comes into question if an officer first observes the vehicle parked, on the side of the road etc. The person may be inside or outside the vehicle, and a police officer and prosecutor need to lean more heavily on circumstantial evidence than in Sarah's case.

So, let us move onto an examination of the impairment or intoxication of Sarah. Speeding alone is not enough to arrest someone for drunk driving, but as Sarah continues to speak and exits the vehicle, the officer builds his case. It should be noted that the officer does not need to offer Miranda warning at this point as it is still an ongoing roadside investigation; as long as evidence of a possible crime continues to present itself, the officer can carry-on.

Only when Sarah is in police custody would statements, she makes be protected by the law. In many cases drunk driving cases, the statements of the Defendant are not the main evidence; the main evidence is usually seeing the person driving and the chemical tests to follow. The one type of case where it may be more relevant is when a Defendant eventually admits to driving if there is not an independent eyewitness to the driving.

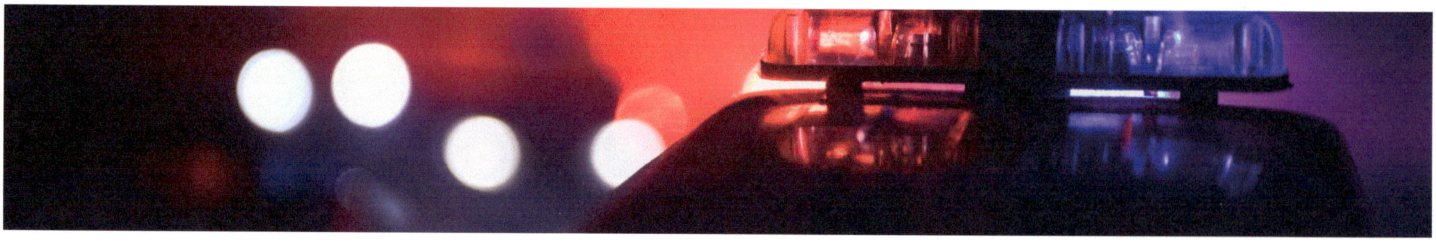

While still inside the car, Sarah provides her information to the officer, and admits to leaving a restaurant with friends; she admits to having 2 mixed drinks, but she feels fine. She admits she was lost and should not have been speeding, but she wanted to get home.

At this point an officer can ask Sarah to exit the vehicle. The officer has evidence she was driving and had consumed alcohol prior to driving. The officer will observe Sarah exit the vehicle and note any trouble exiting, leaning on the vehicle. Officer is observing her speech and her appearance; common remarks are slurred speech, watery and red eyes; you see those in most reports by default.

Once Sarah is out of the vehicle, the officer had her do three field sobriety tests; he performed the horizontal gaze nystagmus test, the walk-and-turn and the one-leg stand; those are the three recognized standardized tests; any tests outside of those are not standardized and should not be a basis of determining the arrest.

Sarah believes she did OK on the tests but had sandals on and was nervous; I explain to her that its rare for anyone to do well on those tests and to not worry about it too much. We will be able to get the officer's report and review any associated audio and video from the tests. While the field sobriety tests can be hit or miss, they are typically used as the basis of the arrest, and most judges would uphold the arrest if the officer followed protocol on the tests.

Officers vary in how well they administrator the tests, and I have found the horizontal gaze nystagmus to be the most fruitful to challenge as officer's rush the test and do it wrong. The audio and video allow us to see and hear what happened; the video can be helpful for the other two, but sometimes they are performed off camera or it is hard to see the feet of my client.

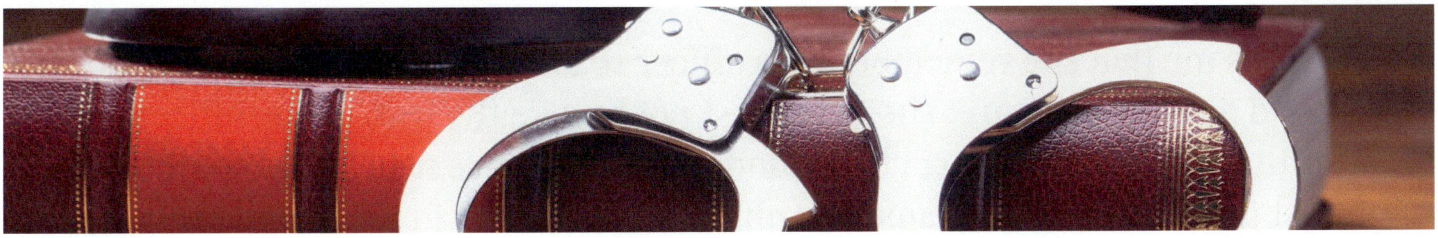

The most important part of the client being outside of the vehicle is whether they performed the Preliminary Breath Test or as it is referred to as the PBT. Clients get confused about the different tests and if they need to take them. Some officers push the PBT on the client and make them think they MUST take the test. Technically by law you do need to take a PBT if an officer believes you were driving and drinking alcohol, but failure to do so is merely a civil infraction, punishable by a fine and 0 points. For those under 21, there are 2 points attached.

Either way, a PBT result for Sarah could make or break the officer's ability to arrest her. While the PBT is not admissible at trial, it can be used as a basis of arrest to examine the probable cause. The PBT test is not deemed reliable enough to be used to determine guilty or innocence, but prosecutors use it as the main tool to uphold an officer's decision to arrest. In Sarah's case, she agreed to take the PBT and the result was 0.14 which is over the legal limit.

The one benefit of the PBT is if you believe you will pass, an officer may send you on your way if under the limit; he/she can still arrest you for being under the limit based on the totality of the evidence, but that case would certainly be open to scrutiny. I believe the upside is low if you are not sure if you'll pass; by being over the limit on the PBT, you're going to be arrested, and the cop/prosecutor have very strong evidence of probable cause. Based on what Sarah tells me, it sounds like the basis of arrest was there at the time.

Finally, we move onto the post-arrest and additional chemical tests. Sarah mentioned that she refused the test; when arrested for a DUI in Michigan, there is something called an implied consent, which means by law you must submit to breath or blood; failure to do so could result in 6 points and loss of license for a year. The officer must follow protocol in this situation and make Sarah aware of these consequences and give her an opportunity to agree or refuse.

Sarah tells me that she remembers the officer reading those rights, but she was confused and was not sure; she felt it best not to take the test. Some officers are better than others in helping clients understand that it is usually in their best interest to take the test, because the officer is going to get results one way or another. By refusing it adds an automatic license suspension to your case. As you will find a ton of information on my website and videos, an implied consent is not the end of the world; there are options, but it certainly complicates the case for Sarah.

Because the officer had to get a warrant for blood, we do not know the result of the BAC and cannot determine what level of charge we will have (Impaired, Intoxicated or High BAC). It is also why her court date is TBD because a date is unlikely to be set before the blood result is back. This could take 10 days or 4 months, it depends on the capacity of the testing lab, how quickly the officer follows up etc.

You can find many articles on my website about challenging breath and blood, but for purposes of this story, we are now going to focus on the Release and Tracking portion of the A-R-T.

As mentioned above Sarah was released on bond by the court. Without prior criminal history, she had to post $300 and promise to come to court when scheduled. She received alcohol testing as a condition of her bond which she must call every morning to determine if its her random day. Sarah must understand the conditions of her release, so she complies from day one. The release portion of a case becomes more complicated when a client cannot post bond, or the judge holds the client to put a tether on their alcohol or some sort of monitoring. Sarah's release was straight forward, and she appears to understand her obligations.

An especially important part of Sarah's case is now the tracking portion; I explain to Sarah that she may not have court for a few weeks, maybe even a month or two. She can sit back and check her mailbox every day; she is likely to lose sleep, be anxious and miserable and she waits for the bomb in her box to show up. This is not a healthy approach to a drunk driving case. Not only is she out of the loop on information, she would waste valuable time doing nothing for her case.

I explain to Sarah that if we work together, we will get things filed with the court, police, and prosecutor; we want to preserve and request all evidence. We do not want video and audio to be deleted or lost, and we want the police and prosecutor to know someone is working with Sarah and keeping her organized and informed. We want to track the status of the blood result and be on top of any warrants or case updates. It is our goal that no warrant for arrest goes into play, and we can simply ask the court to cancel any warrant, and/or waive any arraignment date.

It is our goal to know what is going on, and not to be afraid of the daily trip to the mailbox. It is possible that Sarah misses something, a letter does not arrive, and she sits in limbo as the court begins looking for her; mail and notices get lost all the time. It is better to have a professional tracking the case daily.

Along with information, we want to maximize our time. With a drunk driving case, we will need to overcome the perception that the client is a dangerous drunk driver. It is likely not the first time the person was driving while drunk, but simply the first time they were caught. If a potential client has prior DUI cases, then it is really an uphill battle for the client to overcome that perception.

Our words mean truly little in court, our actions speak louder than anything we can say. I explain to Sarah that if we work together, she would be expected to be proactive from day one. This means likely obtaining a portable alcohol testing device; it would be our goal to test 2x daily and go above and beyond the testing put in place by the court. We would want to change her testing as well, as the portable device will allow a much more convenient method and more dependable and comprehensive.

If we want to change the perception of Sarah, testing 14 times a week, 13 more times than ordered is a good start. We also want to be screened and assessed from a professional in substance abuse; get a basis of where we stand in the present and where we can go moving forward; we usually begin counseling and alcohol education and insight. If a client has prior DUI's, we usually push for intensive treatment, and begin to put in place jail alternatives.

My DUI proactive program is really tailored specifically for each client, with the average client adopting 5 to 6 steps; this will vary by the court, judge, type of charge, prior history and what comes back on the substance abuse evaluation.

Sarah agrees that she wants to take control of her case. She feels terrible about her choice that night; she knows it was NOT a mistake, but a choice. She is motivated by the fact that she could make a positive impact on her case daily with my proactive plan. The alternative sounds unproductive and frankly makes her anxious to think she would be waiting around for the case to smack her on the head. She would lose valuable time and would feel very unprepared

Sarah did not know that this type of approach was possible, but it makes so much sense to be on top of things, and if you want someone to believe in you, you need to earn that from the prosecutor and judge.

I explain to Sarah that if she follows my program and works hard, that she has a major opportunity to change the perception of her case with the prosecutor and judge, and work toward an exceptional result.

As a side note, the Implied Consent refusal must be addressed immediately by my office. Failure to appeal this within 14 days would suspend her license for a year subject to the possibility of applying for a hardship license, which I cover in other writings. Our proactive approach helps tremendously in this issue as well; it may take us into the Circuit Court before a judge who we must request to overturn a Secretary of State license suspension. The weight of that decision should not be taken lightly by a judge, and we must provide the justification for that decision.

Charged with Embezzlement- what are Rachel's options?

Rachel reaches out to me over the weekend about an incident at her former employer. She tells me that she was recently fired and accused of stealing funds from the company. She is unsure of what she may be charged with, but is open and honest about what happened, and deeply regrets her choices.

She tells me that she is 40 years old and worked as a bookkeeper for this company for the past 10 years; she is married with three children and fearful of what is next in the process. I confirm that Rachel has no prior criminal history. I tell Rachel that the offense sounds like Embezzlement, which could be a misdemeanor or felony depending on the value. Anything over $1,000 would be a felony case.

Although Rachel is not yet charged, there is an active investigation and information gathering ongoing by the police department and prosecutor. They are working together with Rachel's former employer on building their case against her. This can be a scary for Rachel with the feeling that the walls are closing in on her from all sides.
I assure her that the police and prosecutor are simply gathering what they can find and will provide Rachel with the same information.

Rachel is most upset because she still cares for and admires all the people who work at her former company, especially the owner. She is beating herself up about how she could portray their trust after so many great years together.

Rachel's first instinct was to reach out to the owner and apologize after she found out she was fired for stealing, but she wanted to talk to an attorney prior to doing so. I praise her for being smart about her choices and advise her that it is not in her best interest to contact her former employer. Reaching out and saying anything could hurt her case and could be construed as witnessing tampering if she says the wrong thing. I assure Rachel that there may be a time and place to make amends for her actions with the employer; she is grateful for this advice and vouches to not contact anyone related to the case.

I walk Rachel through the process of the police and prosecutor working on her case. I assure her that as a former prosecutor, I once sat in that same position, reviewing cases, facts and drafting criminal charges against people. There is nothing personal involved, it's merely a job that needs to get done if there is enough evidence to charge her.

As we discuss what happened, Rachel tells me that as the bookkeeper she was in charge of money coming in and money coming out. She admits that she started using the company credit card for personal items and had them shipped to her home for the last 18 months.

She explains that her husband became ill, could no longer work, but the bills and expenses only went up for three children. She found herself online shopping with small orders then it grew to groceries and more expensive items for gifts for family and friends. She got greedy and figured she had already done something wrong, and it made sense to keep doing it because she was not caught yet.

She admits that in a weird way she was happy that someone caught her, because she could not sleep at night, and kept making it worse. She didn't have an exact number, but she estimates at least $10,000 in personal expenses on the company card. She would simply pay the bill out of the business bank account, and nobody checked her work.

It turns out that she got sloppy with shopping and a large order showed up at the office when she was on vacation with her family. The owner was alerted and after some digging, they discovered her paper trail over many months of spending. The business owner had no choice but to terminate her, which she completely understood.

Rachel is in the unique position that she admits and understand she is 100 percent guilty of breaking the law. She has regret, shame and an angst to make this right for the people she harmed. She is tempted to throw her hands up, beg for forgiveness, and apologize for being a terrible person.

I explain to Rachel that her feeling this way is very normal, and there is a path to making things right, apologizing and possibly rebuilding her past relationships later down the road.

It's important for Rachel to know that right now she is simply a name and a charge on a case file. A prosecutor has no context for what happened; in their mind, she is a cold-hearted criminal ripping off and stealing from others. They are not aware of her underlying issues with family and financial hardship; this is not a defense or an excuse, but it is part of the reason. They may not know she worked there for ten years, and was an outstanding person and friend to the owner prior to lapsing into this dark place in the last 18 months.

When I work with a client like Rachel, it's very clear that she is not a bad person, she is not someone who would ever go out and hurt someone. She let her current financial situation and the stress of her family well-being interfere with her better judgment; she became selfish and wanted a quick fix. She believed that her company made plenty of money, and "nobody would get hurt".

Reflecting back, she realizes that she should have talked to her boss about a potential raise or an advance in pay; by taking matters into her own hands, she has put herself and her family in an even worse spot. Rachel knows that she can't go back in time and undo what she created, but after discussing things in length, she is ready to take control of her case, and change the perception of the situation.

This theft is the first impression for the prosecutor and judge; it is now our turn to create what I like to call a "true impression". A true reflection of who Rachel has been prior to this event, what she is doing in the present to learn, reflect and grow, and what her future goals are moving forward.

Rachel agrees that taking control of her situation will both benefit the outcome of the case and bring her tremendous peace of mind and confidence daily. Dealing with this case daily is taxing, demanding and feels like an endless pit of torture. Charged with a felony is bad enough on its own, but to have hurt and wronged someone you cared about in the process. It's not a good look to make yourself "the victim" in all this, but for someone like Rachel life got out of control and it caused her to act in a manner which is not part of her soul and character.

Rachel agrees to begin my proactive program and tracking plan. We make it a goal to get in contact with the OIC (Officer in Charge) and get information about the investigation. We want to see where things are with potential charges, and hopefully be an active participant in the process. We may or may not add our own statements or information, but we certainly want to be on top of it, and make it clear right away that we indeed to comply with any warrants or charges.

Rachel has a family to think about, and she would live in fear each day that the police would come to her home and arrest her in front of her kids and her sick husband. By working with the police, we would be able to arrange to walk into court and see the judge; there is no need to come find Rachel and arrest her.

We want to begin the case on a good note and earn favorable bond conditions. We don't want to be locked away during the case, posting $10,000's for a bond, or wearing a tracking device. By voluntarily complying and making things smooth for the police, prosecutor and court we stand a much better chance of earning these favorable conditions and sleeping better at night knowing we have some control over the next steps.

In past cases, on an extremely limited basis, we were able to come to an out of court agreement with the police and victim for embezzlement cases. The most likely result are felony charges for Rachel, but with the right officer, prosecutor and business owner, there is a small chance reimbursement can happen without even being charged. We want to at least have this conversation to see what is possible.

Along with tracking the case and actively participating in the dialogue, we want to get proactive. We want Rachel to use this downtime to work on her mental and emotional health; working with a counselor would be the first step. We need to focus in on the underlying issues and begin making progress on coping skills and problem solving methods outside of hurting yourself; exploring that feeling that she is glad she was caught, because she could not stop.

The last impression we want to give a judge and prosecutor is the client is a wild-card; someone who broke the law, but does not understand why or how they ended up there. Without that knowledge and understanding, the client is bound to repeat the same behavior.

If we can provide context, understanding and a thoughtful plan moving forward, we can provide some confidence in a judge and prosecutor that we understand the WHY, and we are working on avoiding returning to that dark place, and if we do return, we know how to handle it in a way that does not end up breaking the law.

Along with counseling, we also want to engage in positive outcomes in our community. While we cannot yet make amends to the business owner, we can make a positive influence on the same County or City impacted by our offense. Rachel will be spending a few hours each week giving back to the community; she is already busy, stressed and overburdened by life, but she is putting that to the side for a few hours and thinking outside of her bubble.

Focusing on her needs, problems and stressful life brought her to this case; by going out into the community and helping others even less fortunate than her, it will assist her in coping with her situation, and hopefully appreciating what she does have, versus what she does not.

For Rachel to come to court with 50 hours logged despite her limited time and energy, it really sends a strong message to the judge and prosecutor.

Ultimately our goal will focus on an opportunity to keep a felony off Rachel's record. If we are able to get the prosecutor, judge and victim onboard with an outcome of redemption, repayment of money stolen and a chance to avoid a felony record and jail, we will have to strongly consider peace of mind and reaching those goals.

Michael is charged with a felony, what can he do?

Michael reaches out to me over the weekend about some felony charges. When a potential client is charged with a felony, we have a more urgent timeline, because felony offenses have a ticking clock for a preliminary examination.

I ask Michael to send me any court paperwork in his possession, which will allow me to see the charges, the court, the judge, when the offense happened, and any bond conditions in his case. It is important to make sure that Michael understands his obligations, the rules for his case, and an idea of potential next steps.

It turns out that Michael is charged with a number of felonies in relation to breaking into property of another, with allegations he had a dangerous weapon, and there was a brief confrontation with the homeowner, which lead to felony assault charges. As a former prosecutor, I understand that a prosecutor will charge as many offenses as possible upfront.

I ask Michael to provide me background on himself, including age, education, work history, family, and any prior criminal history. Michael tells me that he has some juvenile cases back in the day but is not sure of the charges; we make a note to obtain this record going forward.

I learn that Michael is a recent college graduate with a 3.5 GPA, and has plans to apply for jobs in the near future; he comes from a stable family with two parents, siblings, and otherwise is on a good track in life.

As a former prosecutor, I explain to Michael that the prosecutor and judge will view his case from the four corners of the reports. He will viewed as a dangerous young man who showed up at someone's house with a weapon, and things could have ended up with someone killed. You do not get the benefit of the doubt when you enter someone's property with a gun and get into a confrontation.

Michael hearing this is fearful of his future, because having multiple felonies on his record will deter his ability to thrive and survive going forward. Although Michael is off to a bad start with perception of his case, we now explore what the heck he was doing on this evening, and to provide the context and reasons behind it.

Although these facts have created a bad first impression, we now need to explore the possibility of creating a true impression for the prosecutor, and judge in order to work away from worst case scenarios. Without further context of this incident, it will be difficult to create a path for a reasonable resolution.

Michael explains that the house belonged to one of his friends who had some personal items that he had taken from Michael. After digging more into the story, it sounds like Michael showed up in the middle of the night and was trying to retrieve his golf clubs from the other person's garage.

He agrees that he was not invited over, or had permission to do so, but Michael had won a bet, and he was supposed to receive the golf clubs. He was able to access the garage, and while looking around, the other boys parents woke up and confronted him in the garage with a baseball bat; Michael threw a golf club at the other person and ran out of the garage.

I explain to Michael that these circumstances don't necessarily create a defense to "win his case" but it does help us provide context to a prosecutor and judge; this was not a random act, he didn't bring the dangerous weapon with him, and he did not initiate the "violence".

For sure Michael broke the law, potentially in multiple ways, but his presence there was justified in his mind (good intentions?), and his goal was to avoid interaction with the homeowner and leave with property be believed was rightfully his own. While this version of the case may be something to explore at trial, we make it a goal to create alternative outcomes.

The ideal outcome for Michael would be a path to having no criminal record from this case, a chance of dismissal, but a period of time to reflect, and learn that his made a stupid choice to break into someone's garage in the middle of the night to retrieve property. He made it even worse by throwing a dangerous object at someone when confronted and running away.

Some may say, well how was he going to get his property back? At 22 years old, this plan seems like a good idea; the goal is to learn that this is NOT the way to handle conflicts with other people even if justified in your mind. There are other means, maybe more complicated, time consuming and "annoying" but ways to handle it without threatening your entire future. Michael agrees that working toward a solution where he can make amends, apologize, learn, but also potentially earn a great outcome makes the most sense for all parties.

This plan all starts with a timeout and taking a few steps back. We need to reframe this case from dangerous burglar to "stupid kid trying to get his property back from another stupid kid". And I use that casual language on purpose; there is a tendency to apply stiff words and legalese to all cases, especially felonies.

Legally speaking this looks like a profoundly serious case on paper, but reframing it in more casual, easier to digest terms, takes some of that heat off the case, and bridges the gap to a reasonable outcome. If we can get the prosecutor to see this as two stupid kids fighting over a set of golf clubs, my client becomes a lot more human, reasonable, and someone you may want to better understand, and give a second chance.

Reframing the case only begins here, we now need to show that Michael is not this "stupid kid" all the time; this is not a pattern of bad choices or a prediction of future actions. We agree that taking a few proactive steps will be to our benefit in showing who Michael really is; the ambitious young man with a strong GPA, community involvement and big plans.

We agree that the foundation to our entire plan begins with establishing a relationship with a counselor, especially if we can find a counselor that works with younger clients. We want to start a strong relationship where Michael can be open and honest about his emotional and mental health. At 22 years old, we don't have all the answers; I tell him that even at 45, we don't have those answers, and that's ok, but we need to express what's on our mind, and resolve conflict in responsible ways. Michael agrees to research a good counselor to begin working with.

Next, we want to establish and reaffirm that Michael is a positive member of his community; he has a history of community service, but we want to reengage; essentially fill up our calendar so much in the present that we are too busy to get in trouble. We need to counteract the moment where he stepped into that garage, and involved a homeowner, police, prosecutor and court. Any hour we give back to the same community, helps us put positive vibes into the situation.

The most important element of this entire plan comes down to getting the homeowner onboard with the plan. Michael cannot have any contact with the homeowner, and I remind him of that condition, but the prosecutor will speak to the homeowner, and can communicate all the proactive things that we are doing. The prosecutor can also investigate beyond what is in the police report. The reports by the police are created to prosecute, not to give a balanced two-sided account with context.

By having a good relationship with the prosecutor, I can get them to dig a bit deeper into the case and see what is going on with the golf clubs. The prosecutor can also review our counseling progress and community service work. We are also willing to pay any restitution for any damage during the incident; we want to work this out but need the "victim" in the case to agree.

By calling a timeout, regrouping and reframing the case for the prosecutor, she was willing to do some legwork for us. It turns out that the young man who resided at the home admitted to his parents that he did have a bet with Michael, but he didn't think the result was fair, so he refused to give them to Michael.

This confirmation is not a defense for Michael, but it is a confirmation that at a minimum there was a dispute over the ownership of the clubs, and Michael had a reasonable argument of ownership. It makes Michael seem a bit more reliable and reasonable in his actions; still against the law, but potentially closer to justified in his intent.

This confirmation does not excuse the breaking into the garage or throwing a golf club, but it does show this was not a random act, and it's likely to be isolated in nature; Michael had a reason to be there, even though he did it in an illegal fashion.

This does not create a scenario where the prosecutor apologies to Michael, and drops the case, because those results are not common, and should not be expected; Michael overreached his legal ground.

What it does create is a path to a reasonable solution for all parties; potentially a path for charges to be reduced and dismissed. A path where Michael can stand before a judge, admit his poor choice, and actions, but an agreement that is approved by homeowner, prosecutor and judge.

Michael will have a long way to go before he is out of the woods but can straight in a place where he has a second chance to have no record and stay out of jail.

Based on reframing the case, providing context, confirmation by homeowner, and Michael's willingness to be proactive, this outcome is very realistic based on my experience as both a prosecutor and defense lawyer.

Cleaning up Steve's past, and providing a fresh start

Steve reaches out to me about an old felony case from his earlier days. He tells me that when he was in his mid-20's he got caught up with the wrong crowd and ended up doing some foolish things with his life.

Steve has a felony assault on his record and a marijuana charge from two different courts. He has had these on his record for over 10 years and is looking to put his history behind him.

These old cases have become more prominent in his life because he is looking to start his own business, and he may have issues with both a felony and a drug charge on his background check.

Steve's story is quite common in my experience. People have a rough patch in their life, move on and have some success, but a ceiling in their professional life. It is not easy to advance and reach your goals with felony and drug charges on your criminal history.

Even though Steve is now a different man with a family, responsibilities, and no legal issues in over 10 years, his background tells a different story. The reality is nobody cares about your present with a history; they simply do not want or cannot give that person what they deserve.

If Steve can expunge these charges off his record, they will no longer come up in background checks, and his past will cease to exist to the outside world. That sounds like an amazing outcome for Steve, but how do we get to that goal?

Why should a felony assault and a marijuana charge simply go away? What is the standard and process for reaching this goal? Michigan says an expungement decision must be made within the context of "is it in the best interest of society?"

A judge must decide the merits of Steve's request vs the outside world being "warned" and "informed" of his past. Is it worth allowing Steve to put NO CRIMINAL RECORD on an application? Is that the right thing to do for the company, agency or parties reviewing this information?

Steve is rightfully concerned that his past will forever haunt him, and nobody will give him the benefit of the doubt, so why would a judge? Best yet, it will be the same judge ten years later if still on the bench; it will also be the same prosecutor who charged Steve. The Attorney General also gets to weigh in, and the Michigan State Police.

Steve needs the judge, two prosecutors and the police to all agree to this outcome? That sounds like a steep hill to climb, but with the right plan and approach, anything is possible. I make sure Steve understands the hurdle we need to climb, but based on our conversation and the information he has provided me, I determine that he is a good candidate for this type of consideration.

The most important part is Steve does qualify for expungement. Steve has waited enough time since getting off probation (5 years) and qualifies in the amount of charges (1 felony max, 2 misdemeanor max). Just because he qualifies does not mean he is entitled to anything.

We need to take a very humbled and realistic approach to the situation. We also need to be mindful that nobody is in a rush to grant this relief; expungements take months, sometimes a year plus depending on the court, judge, and unique situation.

We also need to be proactive in our approach and do our best to highlight his growth over the past ten years, and his future. We need to focus in on that "best interest of society" for all the key players to review. We need to show that Steve had made legitimate change and the reason for the expungement makes sense for the community.

Steve agrees that it would be in his best interest to take a comprehensive and proactive approach to his case. We begin to work together on having both charges expunged. Steve's case is unique in that the cases are from different courts with different prosecutors and judges; we need to keep all these different players in mind.

The first step is having Steve go back in time and re-examine the person he was back when these incidents happened. There is nothing to hide, the more details, information, and knowledge we can convey to the judge and prosecutor about Steve from ten years ago the better.

We then need to highlight and detail all the positive steps in Steve's life over the past ten years. This includes new education, jobs, family, qualifications/achievements, community involvement and other positive moments in his life.

We need to show Steve at Point A ten years ago, and the timeline he traveled to Point B now. What does that journey look like? Once we flush out this journey, we need to then highlight Steve going from Point B to Point C. That final point is where Steve is planning to go with his life; what is his next big step that he is being held back from?

It must answer the question, if we expunge these cases, now what? Is Steve simply going to sit at home and be the same guy, or is there a next step in his plan?

Because Steve is starting his own business and would be disqualified from receiving licensing because of his past, we need to highlight this as part of his application. Make sure that this barrier is flushed out and clear to the people reviewing his case. We then need to show IF he can start his business, what does this mean for Steve, his family, and the rest of the community?

If Steve has his business open, are those benefits going to outweigh the downside of clearing his past from his history?

Once we have established the answer to the "best interest" question, we now need to shift our attention to what else can we do to enhance our application? Is there something we can do to give more confidence to the decision maker that the best decision is agreeing with our request?

For expungement cases, I like to add two unique elements to my client's application. I like my client to be productive during the time of application, which might mean some community service work in the same city/county as the original case. I want to be able to show the prosecutor and judge that my client is still making amends for his/her past choices and has a strong interest in making the community better. It simply cannot hurt to do more; it may be that little extra gets the job done.

Next, we want to assist the judge in making the ultimate decision. The prosecutor(s) get to object, agree or leave the decision in the judge's discretion, but ultimately the judge makes the final call if the client is eligible. If the judge is going to put his/her neck out there and clear my client's record, we want to assist that decision in our favor.

We do this by having Steve meet with a third-party mental health counselor; someone who can sit down with Steve review the past ten years and make a recommendation if Steve is in the right mindset to move forward with his life. Based on that evaluation, is Steve someone who is likely to offend again, or has he made real changes?

Having a licensed mental health care professional recommend that Steve is prepared to move forward, and is a changed person, can give the judge confidence to simply "follow the recommendation". If someone where to come back to the judge one day down the road and ask for justification for his/her decision to expunge, they can point to my client's third-party recommendation as a foundation for that decision.

Because Steve has provided a detailed ten year timeline which shows his evolution as a member of society, and he's agreed to do the extra community service, and sit down with a neutral third-party professional, he has put himself in a great position. We can now make a compelling argument to the judge why expungement is in the best interest of society.

Peter is arrested for resisting arrest, what can we do?

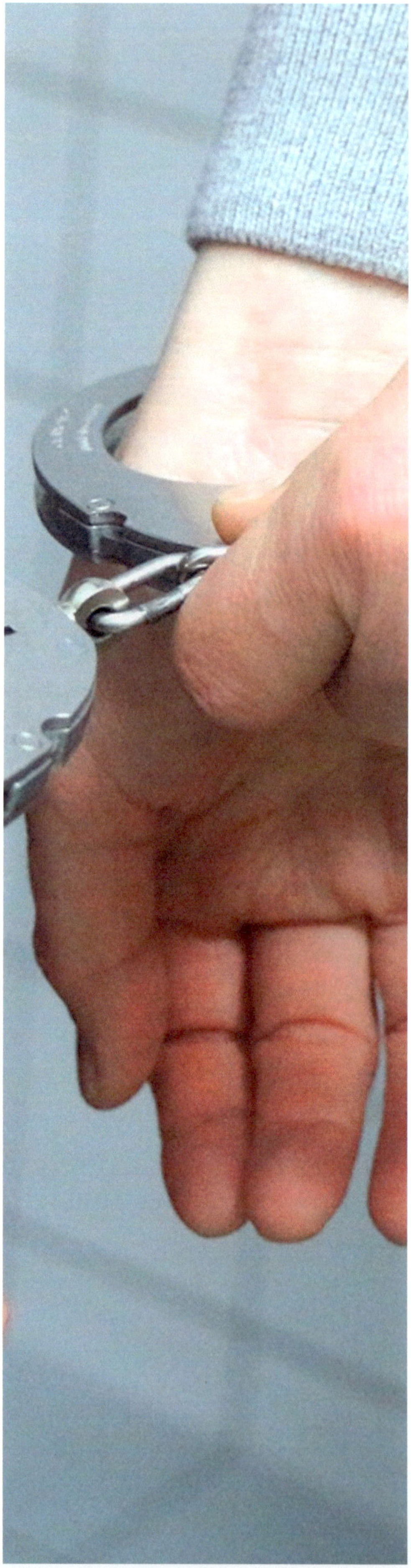

Peter leaves me a voicemail early Saturday morning about a recent Resisting Arrest incident. He says that he was out drinking at a bar with his friends and got into a dispute with one of the bouncers; he was forced to leave the bar and pushed out onto the street.

He felt this was unfair and tried to re-enter the bar; he was denied, and the police were called to the scene.

Some of the details are fuzzy, and Peter is still terribly upset about a situation which he believes was not his doing. He is upset at the bouncers and the police department. Peter is in a very emotional state and has the fight or flight mindset impacting what he is telling me about the case.

I want to be respectful of Peter's version of the story, but it is my job to figure out what the evidence is, not how Peter views what happened.

As a former prosecutor, I view cases from both sides, and understand that a prosecutor only cares about the four corners of the police report. It's also important to focus on the underlying facts of the criminal charge, not use all of our energy and effort on disputing something the client is not even charged with; here is what I mean:

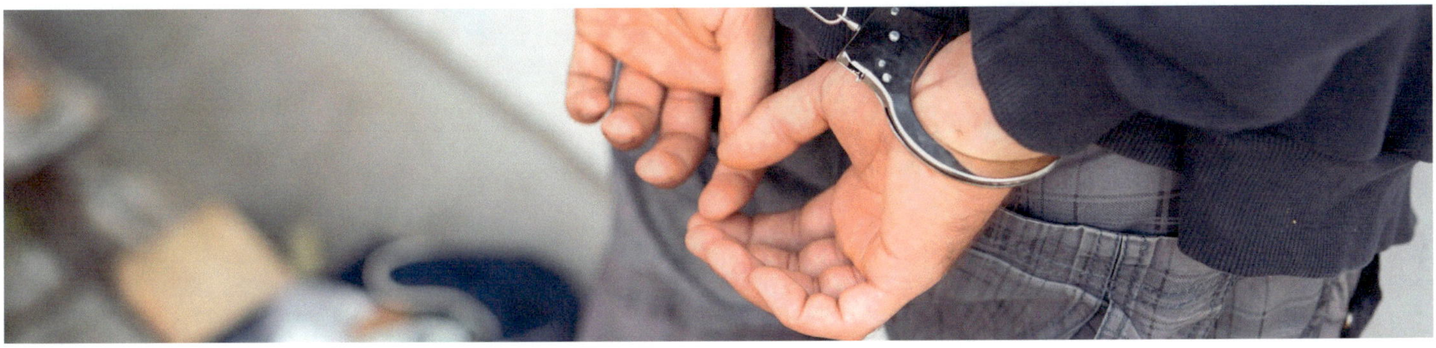

Peter is recounting things that happened in the bar with the bouncer, something about bad service, a bartender giving him the wrong drink, and being unfairly kicked out of the bar. It sounds like he had a bad night, and maybe got some bad customer service. The problem with this is Peter is NOT charged with being kicked out of a bar; it's what is upsetting him, but he's actually charged with shoving a police officer.

Peter wants to focus on the "unfair" part, and not on the crime he committed. This is quite common for a client who is still fresh off the incident; they also tend to focus in on what they believe has two versions of the facts.

Sure, Peter could have valid points about bad customer service, he may even have a civil lawsuit against the bouncer if he was injured, but that is not my focus. My #1 and only focus is the felony charge of Resisting Arrest that Peter is now facing. The extra noise around the case is relevant to an extent, but NOT part of the equation for negotiations or at a potential trial.

If Peter is willing to refocus his energy, insight, and effort into the portion of the facts that landed him charged with a felony then we can get to work on figuring this out. Peter acknowledges that from what he remembers, he did push the police officer, but he says he was really drunk and upset. Once he realizes that the case is all about THE PUSH, he begins to settle down, and is admittingly regretting this poor choice.

I do not want Peter to get too down on himself, I want him to understand the major opportunity presented in this case. Peter has no prior criminal history; he has a good job and a family he loves.

If handled correctly, we can isolate this moment in time, and explore the REASON this happened, not an excuse. We can't use him being drunk as an excuse or a defense, but it appears it was one of the underlying reasons why he acted in a manner, which does not reflect his past.

The problem we face are those four corners of the police report. The prosecutor is going to review the officer and bouncer statements and read about a drunk man causing trouble at a bar; when the police were called, he then shoves a police officer. We have drunk, causing a scene and trouble for a business and assaulting a police officer. Although not charged with being drunk or anything with the bar, these are just pile-on bad vibes for the case.

We deal in perceptions with the prosecutor and judge, and this is a terrible first impression for Peter. The four corners of the police report will sink Peter if we don't do anything to counteract this perception.

Remember when Peter was upset and arguing about what happened inside the bar? I explain to Peter that we're going to turn this negative that he is so mad about, and wanted to "fight it" and turn it into a positive for our case.
We need to make sense of this case for the prosecutor and judge and isolate what happened. We aren't going to dispute it, because he's not charged with doing anything inside the bar, but we are going to flush out he underlying facts that ended up with an officer being pushed by Peter.

We're going to rely on the fact that Peter was drunk and upset to help our case; the more drunk and upset he is, the better for our case! That might not make sense at first, but we need to explain why someone without a criminal record, or any history of issues would push a police officer outside of a bar. This can't be his usual Friday night activity; causing scenes and pushing cops. We don't fight these facts, we use them with the prosecutor and judge to our advantage!

If Peter is so drunk and made, his decision to push the police officer makes more sense. Peter respects the law, and his own father is a retired police officer; if he were sober, or drunk, but not upset, there is no way he would push the police officer.

Of course, we can't go as far as to use these circumstances as a "free push the cop" card but if we can explain the underlying issues, we can isolate the result. Well now what? Every time Peter gets drunk or upset, he is going to break the law?

Well no, Peter is 45 years old and has never had a criminal issue before. But is this a new thing for him? If it is, what can we do about it?

As we explore the issue more it sounds like Peter has been having issues with his wife and was out to blow off some steam. That steam resulted in getting so drunk that he lost control of his better judgment and being drunk and forced to leave the bar put blinders on his decisions. If we can properly address this new underlying issue, we can avoid the #1 worst thing to be at the courthouse.

We do this by being proactive and turning this negative night for Peter into a positive time of growth, reflection, and insight. If Peter is willing to put himself out there, get help and be open to making changes, I am confident that the prosecutor and judge will better understand his actions, and agree to support our long-term goals for Peter.

Peter agrees that the best approach is to take control of his case in a proactive way. He also agrees that his drinking in past few weeks has accelerated and his stress level is way up. He was drinking in order to get through the tough days and nights and agrees that he could use professional help.

I am proud that Peter is open-minded about getting this proactive help, and better understanding of his mental, emotional, and physical health. This process will begin with professional counseling to address the stress and anxiety issues; we also need to address the new substance abuse problem developing.

It is also important to address the "anger management" issue from the push; while Peter may not have an issue with anger as a whole, but in a particular moment his brewing anger ended up in a felony charge. We are going to be humble and be open to all help for this case.

We also want to demonstrate that Peter is a productive member of our community; this comes with highlighting his career, education, and family, but all of that was in place when he pushed the officer; we want to do something new.

We decide to sign-up for community service hours in the same community where this incident happened. We want to give back positive energy and put in sweat equity. We have a case where we disrupted a local business and respected and assaulted a member of law enforcement. We cannot change what happened, but we can certainly do our best to counteract the negative energy which the incident; it is a start, and only helps our position.

Because Peter has agreed to be proactive, we now have a path to create an outstanding result in his case. Both the result itself, and setting him up to succeed in the future, with his family, career, and his overall well-being.

Peter's progress will be shared with the police officer, prosecutor, and judge; there are the key players that we need to look beyond the four corners of the police report.

It is our goal to work toward avoiding a felony on Peter's record and avoiding jail time; those are our two main goals, and both can be accomplished because of Peter's decision to be proactive.

We shifted Peter's mindset of anger, frustration and feeling like a victim to a humbled and reasonable mindset that focused on tangible goals with a comprehensive plan to reach them.

Courtney violated her probation, what can we do?

Courtney reaches out to be about a drunk driving case, indicating that she failed to do some testing, and must go see the judge in two weeks. I reach out to Courtney for some clarification on her legal issue, as what is she is explaining could be two different things: a bond or a probation violation.

A bond violation occurs prior to sentencing, while a probation violation happens when you have already been sentenced, and currently on probation; for Courtney, it turns out to be a probation violation.

I ask Courtney for a series of information, including her original sentencing terms of her case, the court, the judge, her probation officer's name, and any paperwork or order received from the court indicating the allegations of her violation.

It turns out that Courtney received the default/standard drunk driving sentencing, because she did take any proactive steps with her attorney. I explain to Courtney that her original sentence appears to be pretty standard, but I provide her a little background on what she would have done if we worked together initially, and how we could have shortened her probation, and many of the terms which are now giving her issues while on probation.

Courtney is upset that things detoured and explains that she simply did not really understand how her testing worked, and her obligations to the court. She wishes she had been proactive and more on top of things earlier in the case but appears open to making some changes.

It turns out that Courtney was placed on random testing for both drugs and alcohol; she has had no issues with drug testing for the first four months of probation but has various alcohol test violations. Some tests she failed to appear for, a diluted sample and one positive test.

When placed on probation for something as serious as drunk driving, the judge is giving you a second chance in not sending you to jail. A chance to go on probation, comply with sentencing, and work on a series of steps in hope that you do not put yourself and others in danger again.

I typically have clients accomplish many of these steps during their case with the goal to avoid them being part of the sentence, because it opens pitfalls and opportunities to violate even with the best intentions.
I explain to Courtney how the judge and prosecutor now view her case.

She was given a chance to comply and succeed, but now she's testing positive for alcohol, potentially trying to "game the system" with a diluted sample, and showing she is irresponsible and not a dependable trustworthy person who can show up and test.

As a former prosecutor and defense attorney, I've heard it too many times from the judge "there is one place where I know you can't drink, and that's jail"; Courtney is scared by this, but understands that her actions have consequences.

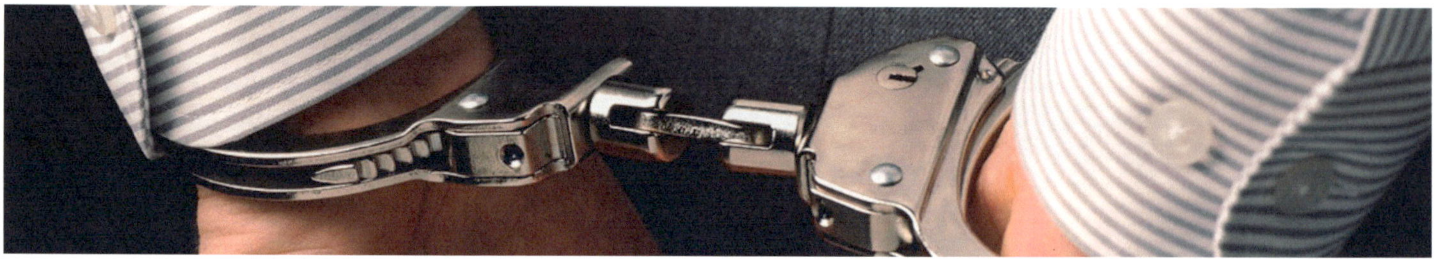

Courtney now has a decision to make; does she want to show up in the court, apologize? Deny? Cry? Not sure? The options are typically not great for someone like Courtney, because she knows that she messed up, and now she wants another chance?

By going in with no plan, you give a judge no choice but to “send a message” and lean toward punishment such as jail, extension of probation and other sanctions. Unfortunately, this is what most people do when they violate probation.

They already have not done anything to impress the judge and prosecutor for their actual case; it was simply a continuation of the incident itself. Now they screwed up again. You cannot blame a judge for throwing Courtney in jail, and the entire hearing becoming an extremely uncomfortable and unproductive day for her.

But what if there was a different approach? We cannot go back in time and be proactive for the initial drunk driving case, but we can take the current situation, and apply many of the same principles.

Courtney is alleged to have done three different things. Drinking alcohol, not showing up for testing and possibly trying to game the system with a diluted sample. I can already hear and see the judge berating her over each issue.

Now that we are working together, and she is onboard with being proactive, we will use the two weeks prior to court in order to better position her case.

The first thing we do is begin using a portable alcohol testing unit. This will not replace her scheduled testing for now, but the goal will be to test above and beyond what is ordered, test perfectly, and ask the court to adopt the new comprehensive testing as her new means to alcohol test.

If one of Courtney's issues was missing tests, being late, and not being responsible, well now she has a testing unit with her at her home, and she has no excuses. It will also make her text 2x daily (14 total tests) vs 2 tests per week.

A judge will be impressed that she stepped up to the plate and solved one of the issues on her own. A judge can also adopt our testing as a sanction; testing 14 times is more than 2, so we can call that a penalty, right? By suggesting the penalty, and self-imposing we are now taking the pressure off the judge to act.

We do not stop here, because she did test positive for alcohol while on probation for drunk driving; that is a serious violation of the judge's trust and violation of a court order. Most judges will impose jail for this violation.

We need to create "jail alternatives" so a judge is not inclined to send Courtney to jail. We do this by self-imposing additional community service hours, and we sign up for a special alcohol weekend program, which 100's of my clients has attended with great success. I send the referrals to Courtney, and she gets both in place.

With only two weeks before court, we may not be able to finish these additional sanctions, but by starting them or signing up, we can let the judge know what we've put in place, and ask for those to be the "punishment".
Because Courtney has followed my plan, we are now in a particularly good position to take the sting off her violation.

Depending on the court, we may send these updates to her probation officer, or wait until she meets with the probation officer the morning of court.

Ultimately the probation officer will recommend something to the judge; we want to influence this recommendation and get the probation officer in our corner. We will have the opportunity to review this recommendation at the courthouse and prepare to address the court.

We will either be asking the judge to follow the recommendation if the probation officer adopts our sanctions or arguing against the recommendation if the probation officer is still seeking jail. Based on my years of experience, if a client steps up like Courtney did, we stand a very good chance of walking out of the courtroom with a deep breath, and a lesson learned that self-reflection and action are the best means for re-taking control of your case.

The worst night of college for Madison - now what?

Madison reaches out on a Sunday evening, and tells me that she has been charged with an MIP. I follow up and ask her to send me any ticket or paperwork from the police officer. I also ask her for a summary of what happened, and a little background on herself.

It is quite common for a young client to mention a single charge, when, they have multiple charges. It turns out that Madison is charged with Minor in Possession, Urinating in Public, possession of a Fake ID and Open Container. Madison is a college student who was ticketed while leaving a tailgate party and going to the bathroom behind a bush next to the sidewalk. She is very embarrassed about the event.

As someone with no prior record, she is concerned about a criminal record, jail, and what happens next with the case. She has not yet told her parents, because she is worried, she will get in trouble, and would rather not get them involved.

First off, I make sure that Madison knows that everything is going to be OK. Without a prior criminal record, she is certainly in a good position to learn from this and move forward in the right direction. It is also important that she understands we have three criminal misdemeanors, and one civil infraction.

We need to acknowledge how a prosecutor and judge will view the case; they do not get the opportunity to meet Madison, and learn about her background, and any future goals. To them, she is someone who was completely out of control on a college campus; underage drinking in public, urinating and possessing a fake ID. To them, this is NOT the first time she's done this, but rather the first time she was caught.

How do they stop this happening again with Madison? Do they need to punish her? Give her a record so others who may wish to hire her know she is a problem child?

As a former prosecutor, I viewed this "college crimes" with a unique prospective. I was once young and dumb and did things that I regret, but for some reason, there are prosecutors who do not think that way. Maybe they did not have a good college experience and hold a grudge against youthful offenders who remind them of their own childhood. It's rare, but I've had prosecutors who want to punish youthful offenders even harsher than adults.

We can't rely on the fact that Madison has never been in trouble, and she is guaranteed a second chance. We need to be proactive, and highlight who Madison was prior to this happening, what she is doing in the present to learn from this incident, and her plans moving forward. Give them a reason NOT to give her a criminal record.

Madison agrees that it would be a good idea to change the perception of her case; being judged on the ticket alone is not an accurate reflection of who she is as a person.

It is important to address the elephant in the room; nobody thinks this was not Madison's first-time underage drinking, and, nobody expects it to her last. She needs to be more aware of her surroundings; if she were more responsible and simply left the party without the urinating and attention, she brought to herself, she may have not been ticketed.

Underage drinking in college is a bit like speeding; most will do it, most will get away with it, but if you're going to go 90 MPH or drive in a reckless way, you're going to be caught and ticketed. For every 10 people in Madison's same situation, 9 walked away without issue, but Madison made it worse with her additional choices.

Now that she has been caught, it's time to learn a valuable lesson, and make this the most serious time she ever walks into a courtroom. I tell Madison that she is fortunate; it may not feel like it in the moment, but if this prevents a worse offense, then it will be worth it. The 9 people who got away with it, may have to learn their lesson with the law with something more serious.

Madison is confident if she follows my proactive program that the prosecutor and judge will be open-minded about a second chance, and redemption.

We start by addressing the alcohol usage; in no way do we consider Madison to be an alcoholic or a problem drinker at this point. We focus on awareness, insight and experience-based learning. We want Madison to focus on making good healthy choices in college; to focus on her grades, and to not jeopardize her own safety. Consuming alcohol in college goes beyond avoiding the cops; drink too much and you can find yourself unaware of your surroundings and be hurt or taken advantage of by another.

Most college campuses have alcohol awareness program geared toward their students; it's usually 1-2 sessions and convenient to accomplish. If the school does not have this program, I refer the client to another program, which will accomplish the same goal. We get a certificate of completion for the program and have made a big step in the right direction.

I also have my young clients attend 1-2 AA meetings locally in the area in order to get a better understanding of "what could happen". My clients are not in a position where AA is necessary and we are likely not at a dependency or sickness, but we never want to be there. If we can learn about the pitfalls of alcohol at age 20, we can avoid those worse case scenarios at 35 or 40 when my clients have careers, families and more to lose.

Madison agrees to sign up for the class at her school, and plans to attend two AA meetings, going once a week for two weeks. We also decide it would be beneficial for Madison to write a letter to herself that she could have put on her nightstand the morning she woke up on the date of her incident.

We can't go back and change what happened, but what would we tell ourselves is going to happen, and why? Hopefully attending the awareness course and some AA meetings will make this clearer to understand. It also helps Madison when we go to court if a judge inquires on why did this happen, and what did she learn form it?

A prosecutor and judge need to hear that Madison understands how she found herself in this situation, and what she is doing moving forward to avoid it happening again, or something worse. There are some judges that see these types of offenses as a gateway to more serious drug offenses, and drunk driving. We want to avoid the client being hammered into deterrence.

Madison shares her letter with me, and she realizes that she drank way too much, didn't pour her own drinks, wasn't aware of how much she drank, and barely ate anything that morning. Because she was at a crowded party at a house, she was not familiar with, she did not feel comfortable using the bathroom. She hoped to find a business to use their bathroom but was not able to do so. She simply had to use the bathroom, and just went.

It is also important that Madison understands how serious possessing a Fake ID is for a potential background check in the future. While most think of a Fake ID as a way to underage drink or get into a bar, the charge will look very different on a background check.

Phrases like fraudulent identification, altered government documents are NOT what you want on a criminal charge on your record. There is no explanation that says "Madison was only 20 and wanted to be 21 to go to her favorite bar".

A grad school, future employer, customs or anyone reviewing it will not have that context. Madison makes sure to address this in her letter to herself and urges her to remove this from her wallet as it is a ticking time bomb. It is important we acknowledge this for a prosecutor and judge.

Madison also agrees that it would be worthwhile to spend two days volunteering with a non-profit in her college town. While she has volunteered in the past, we want something fresh and new; a self-imposed penalty for breaking the law. We need to counteract these criminal charges with some positive vibes of her own.

Because Madison has followed my lead, and agreed to be proactive, she is in an excellent position to resolve her case in a favorable way. Despite three misdemeanors, we can likely create a path to have no criminal record from this incident, and limit court supervision.

Depending on the court, and prosecutor, it may also be possible to avoid the civil infraction for an MIP. While this seems less serious than a misdemeanor, a civil infraction will always be public, and will go on your driving record. I have seen clients have more difficulty explaining an MIP on their record than the original criminal misdemeanors.

Fortunately for Madison, our prosecutor agrees to dismiss all three criminal charges, and the one civil infraction in a view different way, and the judge is agreeable. With such an extraordinary outcome, some judges may question the outcome, but we have justified the deal we received, and all parties are in agreement that Madison has earned a second chance.

David is charged with domestic violence, what are the next steps?

I get an early morning voicemail from David, who has just been released from custody. He informs me that he was arrested for domestic violence and is now staying with his brother. He was told not to return to his home with his wife and kids. David is scared and has a piece of paper with a court date and a list of bond conditions.

He wants to talk and find out what the next steps for his case would be with an attorney.

After reviewing this information, I reach back out to David to learn more about his background, the case, and some goals for the case.

David tells me that the incident involved his wife who he has been married to for 28 years, they have two children, and he has not had any issues with the law since he was much younger; I clarify when and what is in his past, and he tells me an old DUI from about 20 years ago.

David is a consultant to travels often and is the main financial support for his family; he is worried that his wife may divorce him, and he won't be able to see his teenage children.

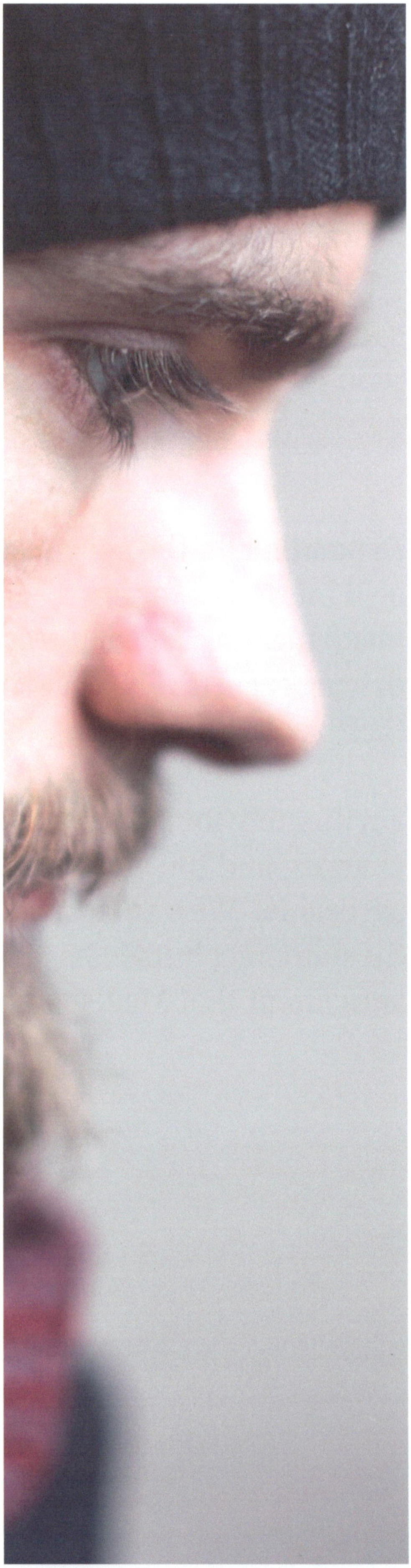

We then discuss what exactly happened; David is honest and says he drank way too much, and he got into a verbal fight with his wife about him not being home enough, and she suspected he was cheating on her while traveling during the week. Eventually this led to his wife swinging violently at him, yelling, and David reacted by shoving her against the wall, which caused her to hit her head. One of the teenage children called the police, and he was arrested.

David is extremely apologetic about his actions, and admits that without drinking, this would not have escalated to violence. He didn't mean to hurt his wife, but she would not stop swinging at him, and he didn't know what to do. He is worried about international travel and his job with a domestic violence offense on his record.

It's very common for clients to assume that if the "victim" wants to drop the case, that it can just go away. For the most part, this is NOT true. A prosecutor prosecutes a case on behalf of their city, town, village or county, not on behalf of the victim; even if the person alleged harmed wants the case to go away, that is not their decision.

I ask David to send me the bond conditions which he was provided, and we go over what the no-contact order means. He must not return to his home, and cannot have any contact with his wife, even via third party. There is nothing on the no-contact order about his children, so he would be able to reach out to them and arrange to see them and talk to them.

David is ok staying with his brother on a temporary basis, but is curious about when he can go home, and I explain that it's a process, and it's not happening just yet.

I explain to David how a judge and prosecutor view his case. In his mind, he drank too much, he took it one step too far, but this has never happened again, his wife ended up being shook up, but unharmed, and he is extremely remorseful. It's easy to think that this can blow over and move on with better intentions.
The prosecutor and judge know nothing about David, and do not take the same approach. They will assume that David is a drunk, a dangerous man, and his violence threatens his family if he returns to the home.

They can see his part DUI history, and while not directly related to domestic violence, it is a history of alcohol and breaking the law. It doesn't help our case that in the police report, David blew a 0.19 BAC on a PBT while in police custody.

David, and I begin to work together, and I file my documents with the court, police and prosecutor so we can receive police reports, statements and any audio, and video. We also want to confirm the first court date, and open lines of communication with the prosecutor.

Once we receive the police reports, we are also provided a copy of a 911 call, which captures some audio from the incident, as one of the teenagers was calling the police on David.

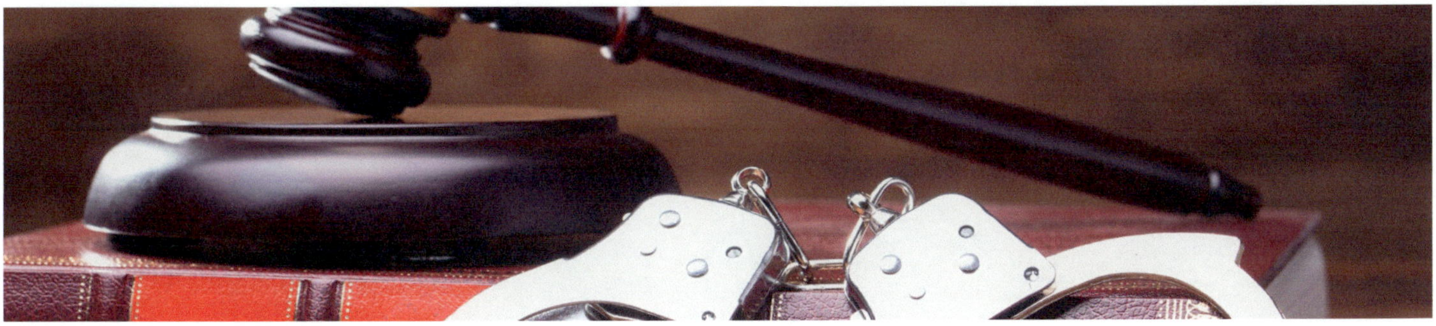

In the 911 call, you can hear the teenager fearful that his dad was going to hurt his mom. More alarming, David threatening to kill his wife; something that David, and myself agree was the alcohol and his frustration peaking, and not his true thoughts or intentions, but again, the prosecutor and judge are going to think very different of these words.

While David maintains that the motivation for pushing his wife was her swinging her arms at him, I explain that the only way to present that theory of the case is at a trial, and that option is on the table, but we need to explore other means of resolution.

Because of his documented intoxication, the teenager calling to report dad as the offender, and the audio of the death threat for any jury or judge to hear, it's not exactly the best case to try in court. David agrees that an alternative resolution may be in his best interest.

I explain that any favorable resolution would need to be approved by a prosecutor, the judge, and most importantly his wife. He is confident that she would be open to working toward a suitable outcome if presented to her. I explain that the prosecutor will likely use a victim advocate to learn of her wishes, and her position on any outcome.

While we have a solid roadmap in place, we now have a lot of work to do in order to change the perception of David's case. A superior outcome is a longshot if we do nothing proactively.

David sees the value in beginning a series of proactive steps on my program. Because of the documented alcohol in David's system, he has been ordered to do random alcohol testing as part of his bond, and we discuss how to comply, but we agree to go above and beyond and begin using a portable breath testing machine. We agree that it's our goal to have the court adopt our more aggressive testing, but for now, he will do both.

We want to show the judge and prosecutor that alcohol is not an underlying issue for David despite his past from 20 years ago. When told not to drink, he can comply, and he is not a threat to get drunk again and hurt someone he loves.

We also agree to begin a proactive program geared toward domestic violence cases, because David admits that he handled the situation poorly, and can certainly learn valuable lessons in deescalating situations; he wants to work on himself, because he's been drinking more than usual, working long hours, and very stressed.

His actions don't reflect how much he loves and respects his wife and children, but his underlying stress and drinking turned him into something he doesn't want to become that evening. If that's the worst incident that happens between him and his wife the rest of his life, he will be grateful, but he admits he needs help, because when he drinks, he can be someone he doesn't want to be.

David is grateful to begin a program with specialized counseling, which incorporates a substance abuse component. I also advise David that I want him to go to a few AA meetings, and get a sense of how alcohol has impacted others.

It's more educational at this point, because I want David to hear from the people who have lost careers, been divorced, lost respect of friends and family because of their drinking.

David also agrees that his actions caused a domino effect of public resources with the police, jail, prosecutor, court and judge all touching his case, because of his poor choice. He believes doing a few days of community service in the same city as his case would be a way to begin to counteract what happened and put positive vibes and energy back into the system.

Within 24 hours of this terrible and regrettable incident, we now have a realistic set of goals to keep domestic violence off his record, avoid jail time, and help him learn from this incident, and be a better husband and father.

We embrace that this happened for a reason; nobody was seriously hurt, and we can turn this into a manageable situation. David understood that words, promises and best intentions don't move the needle, and agreed to a comprehensive proactive approach to the problem.

We are now addressing the alcohol concerns, the conflict resolution and therapeutic issues, and counteracting breaking the law, by giving back valuable time and resources to the same community.

Imagine if David didn't agree to all of this? That's what 99.9 percent of people who are charged with domestic violence do every single day in Michigan. They allow the four corners of the police report to define them, and not a single thing changes when they go to court.

David is now on the path to creating a "true impression" of who he is, and where he plans to go in the future with the lessons learned from this case. He is in an excellent position to reach all of his goals, and return home to his family.

Michael has been charged with Reckless Driving and Leaving the Scene

Michael reaches out to me about several charges on a traffic ticket. He starts by telling me he's charged with Reckless Driving; I ask him to send me the ticket, because most of the time, a ticket has multiple charges listed, and a few issues to discuss.

When I receive the ticket, I see a handful of charges; Reckless Driving, Careless Driving and Leaving the Scene of an Accident.

As I am reviewing the tickets, I ask Michael to give me more information about himself, including past criminal/driving history, background on his family, career, and a summary of what happened.
Michael tells me that he has no criminal history, but a history of speeding tickets, and he works in the auto industry at Ford Motor Company as an engineer. He is single, ambitious and is required to have a driver's license for his position. He was also driving a company car at the time of the incident.

In his summary of the events, Michael tells me that while driving about a mile from his home, he was cut off by another driver. He sped up and chased the other car down; during this chase, both cars ended up colliding and on the side of the road. Both drivers got into a verbal argument, and Michael drove off and went home with the intention of calling the police.

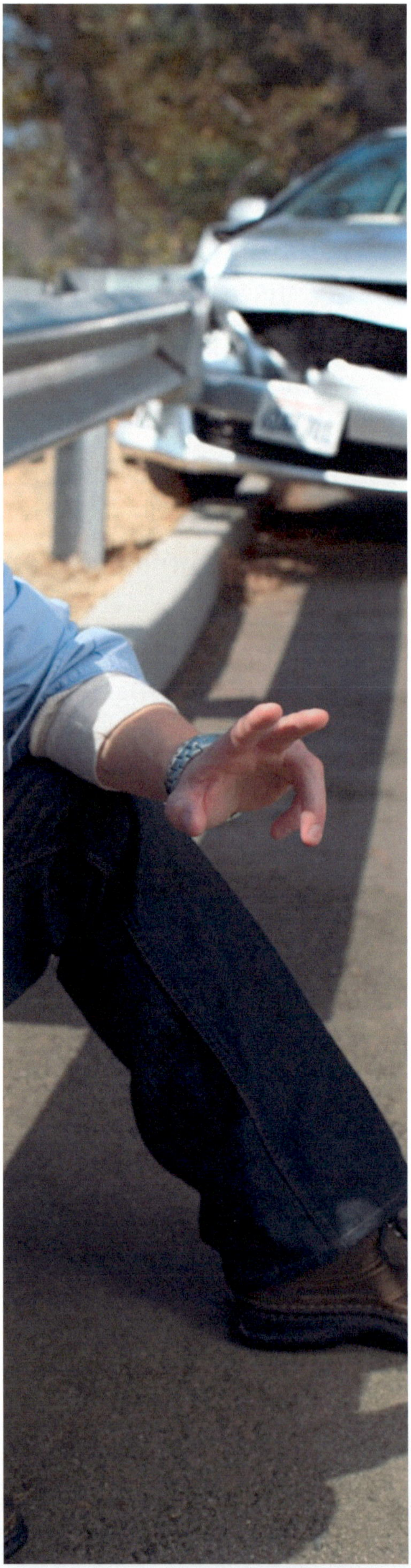

When a client tells me what happened, I understand that it's the best version of their case; meaning, they may leave out some facts, twist some facts for it to sound better. That's ok; it's very natural to have a fight or flight, and sometimes we say what we wish we did, rather than what we did.

I have to strike a balance with a new potential client at this point. I want to be supportive of their version of the story, but it does me no good if I simply say OK, and we go with their version of the story. I find it helpful to ask a series of follow-up questions, because I view every single potential case from both the defense side, and the prosecution, and how a judge would view the case.

Remember, the prosecutor and judge are just going to read the police report; they were not present, and my client does not get to file a defendant's report to read.

Based on what Michael told me, he acknowledges he was out on the road, had some sort of traffic incident with another car, and admits he left, but with the intention of calling the police.

First follow up question would be, did you call the police? Michael says no with a few reasons why he did not; the only key fact there is he didn't call the police; even if he did, he still left the scene of an accident. He tells me he was scared of the other driver, that's why he left; this makes more sense, and is more relevant.

So we have Michael's version, but we won't know the full picture until we see the police report, accident report, and any other evidence. For now, I do my best to educate Michael on the charges.

Some people view a traffic ticket as less serious than "criminal charges"; unfortunately, many traffic tickets are misdemeanors, and they are more serious.

Not only are they potential criminal charges on your record, but they also go on your driving record, give you points, could impact your driver's license, and there are NO dismissal programs for traffic tickets. Under the current law, there is also no way to expunge a traffic offense.

The Reckless driving is misdemeanor, which carries 6 points, and a 90-day hard suspension of your driver's license. This charge has more serious driver's license consequences than drunk driving, the same or more points, and is a misdemeanor.

The Careless Driving is a civil infraction, and 3 potential points on your license. The Leaving the Scene depending on how it is categorized is either 0 or 6 points, and a criminal misdemeanor.

When confronted with multiple charges, I think back to my day's as a prosecutor; we always charged as much as we could to create leverage to make deals. If we only charged one thing, we lose the ability to work something out.

Also relevant to this case is Michael's past driving record for speeding. While by no means a serious flaw in Michael's life, it's strong evidence in the prosecutor's eyes that Michael speeds, and may not be the most cautious driver. For every speeding ticket you receive, you probably get away with it another 99 times.

We have to overcome the "asshole factor" with the prosecutor. Although Michael is a hard-working professional, the prosecutor never gets to meet him, and will only judge him on his speeding record, and this case. A prosecutor creates an image in their head based on their own driving interactions, and people who have upset them, or they've witnessed driving in dangerous ways around them.

Once Michael and I begin working together, we track down the police report, which is completely one sided, because the other driver reported the whole incident to the police and failed to mention their role if any in the incident. Michael is labeled a dangerous driver who chased down the "victim" and was verbally abusive and put the other driver's well-being in grave danger.

Michael certainly has the option of going to trial on all three charges, but there is great risk there. There is no independent witness who can tell the "real story"; it's the guy who was responsible and called the cops vs the guy who allegedly drove off. In order to have any chance of contesting the case, Michael would likely need to testify, which opens up potential additional liability for testifying under oath. It also opens up the door with the judge for potential harsher sentencing.

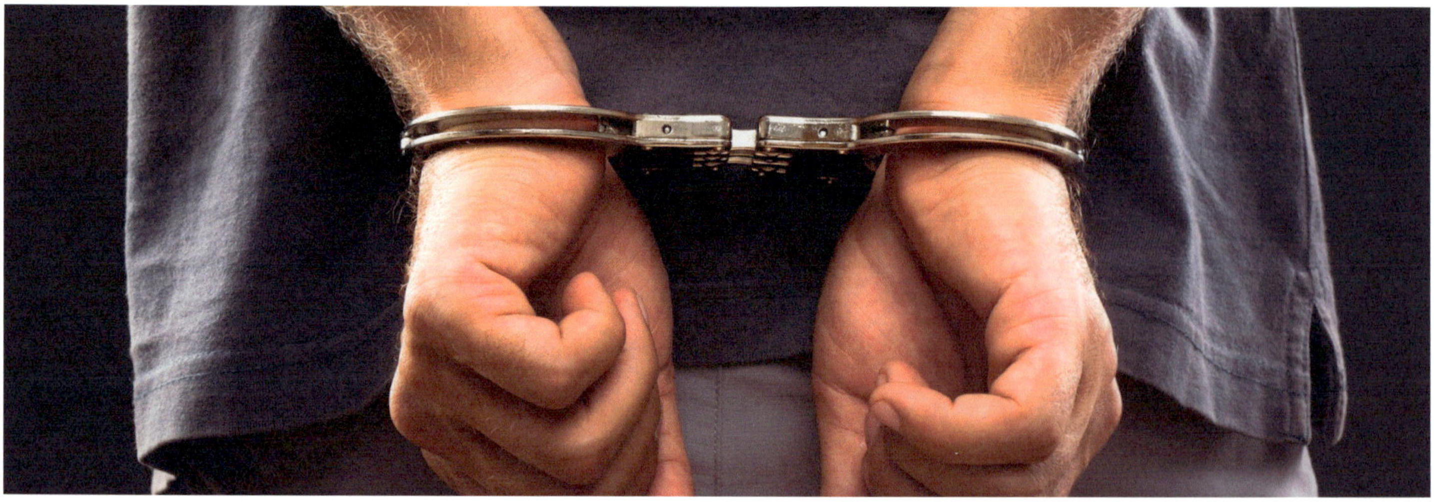

Simply put, if you work out a deal on most traffic offense, a judge is barely going to notice the case, assess some fines and may not even consider probation, and certainly not jail. You make a judge sit through a trial, hear testimony, and all “dirty details”, and you’re convicted, you then get on the judge’s radar big-time.

I advise Michael that we’re going to keep all out options open, but let’s explore best case scenarios. We make it a goal to work toward an outcome, which doesn’t lead to any criminal record, no loss of driver’s license, and no probation.

If we can walk away from this case with our driver’s license, no criminal record, and no court supervision, we agree that we likely would accept that outcome. Unfortunately, we still need to overcome the one-sided facts, and my clients driving record. Here is where we get proactive and change the perception of the case.

I ask Michael to keep an open mind, and even if he disagrees with some of the police report and statements of the other driver, we need to acknowledge that the prosecutor is going to consider that to be the truth in working out any deal. We need to isolate what happened, and work on presented a more in-depth, accurate and fair background on his past, present, and future.

I ask Michael for his resume, so I clearly understand his education and professional success. I also ask him to meet with a counselor one-time to talk about what happened. I understand from my experience, that my client is going to be more open with a professional therapist who is trained to ask the right questions.

Along with this counseling session, I will request a report from the counselor to better help me understand what happened. It turns out that Michael had a bad day at work, and the other driver triggered him. He is remorseful for acting in that way and admits that he could have handled it better.

This is very helpful, because Michael is now in a better mindset, and understand what happened. It helps me provide some context to the prosecutor that Michael isn't a dangerous/irresponsible person, but he is currently dealing with stress at work, and is learning alternative methods to work on these issues such as mediation, exercise, and has breathing techniques to move past these feelings. It's these little angles and insights that help move a prosecutor off their initial feelings on a case.

The fact my client cared enough to meet with a counselor, and I have this official report created on the session. We also back this up with a driver improvement course approved by the State of Michigan, and a day of community of service within the court's jurisdiction.

Michael has demonstrated how serious he is taking this isolated poor choice in his life. He realizes that he should have handled it better; he is humbled by what happened and is ready to resolve the case with our goals in mind.

Because of Michael's proactive efforts, the prosecutor agrees to an outcome of no criminal record and no suspension of his driver's license. I remind Michael not to blame the other driver before the court, accept the reduced outcome and be positive. Because Michael follows my lead, the judge assesses a fine, and warns my client to drive safe, and not come back to his court. Agreed!

Charged with retail fraud, what's the next step?

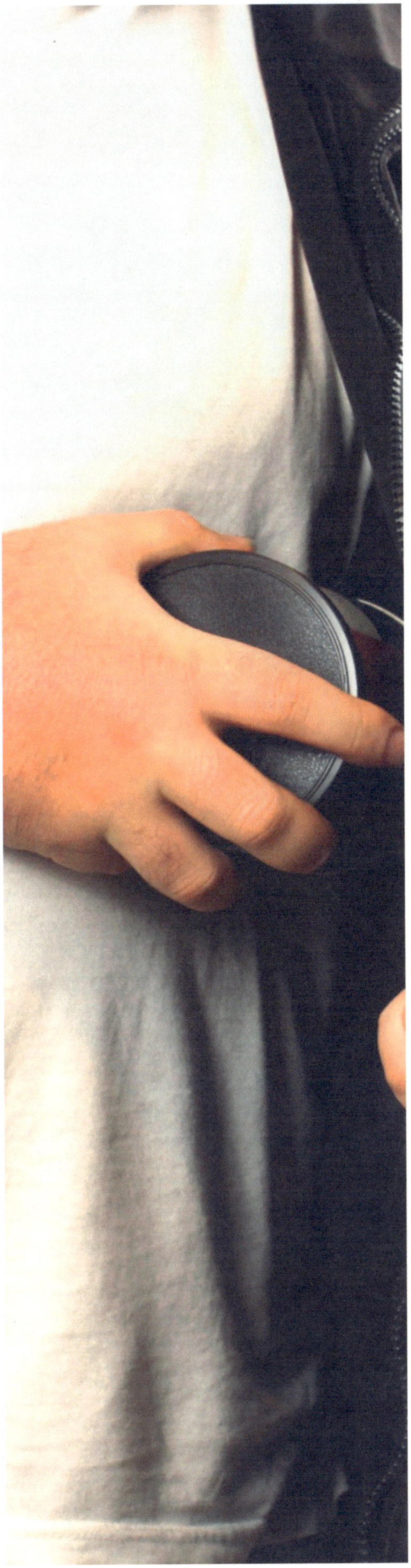

Jennifer reaches out to me about a recent incident while shopping at her favorite department store. Jennifer was arrested for shoplifting some clothing items and charged with retail fraud.

She is recently divorced and has three young children. She has been stressed out at work, along with an ongoing custody battle, but has never been in trouble with the law before.

She tells me that she is a nurse and is very worried that this offense would take away her ability to support her family, and would lose her nursing license, which she worked so hard to earn.

I assure Jennifer that although this is a serious offense, that her future is very much within her control. It's a good sign that she has identified some stress triggers in her life (work and family). I assure her that this sounds like a mental and emotional cry for help, and this is not turn her into a bad person, or a thief.

Although I can identify this common issue from my years of working with retail fraud clients, a prosecutor and judge simply don't agree. It's very common for a prosecutor and judge to see a name and a charge for stealing and assume that my client has been stealing for years and was finally caught. Now that we "got her" she should be punished and given a criminal record.

The first thing I tell Jennifer is that she needs to be aware of all potential reporting obligations to the State of Michigan for her license. I offer to refer her to a professional license attorney if she needs further guidance. Most of my clients who hold professional licenses will speak to this type of attorney outside of our work together to gain additional information.

From there we discuss the stress of the custody battle and her work anxiety; we setup an initial counseling appointment so she can further understand these triggers, and put a plan together going forward. It's not good enough for my client to identify these underlying issues, we need a professional in that field to meet with her, and agree, while putting a plan in place.

We need to work away from that "wild card" factor; we cannot be unreliable to a judge and prosecutor, because they assume Jennifer has been stealing, with no plan to stop despite being charged with a crime.

Having a counselor slow the pace down and meet with Jennifer on a regular basis as we're preparing for court, has now put her on a positive path. We supplement these sessions with support group meetings with other people charged with the same crime.

There is a group here in Michigan, which I recommend for all of my clients to attend. They do in-person meetings, and even meet over Zoom and the phone.

On top of these support group meetings, we put some educational classes into place, which I send these referrals to Jennifer, and she happily signs up. She is able to complete these courses in person or online.

My clients have told me in the past, that they learned a lot, and really understand how big this issue can be in this world, and the impact their small decision has on the greater picture. Jennifer signs up, and has now counseling, support group meetings, and educational classes in place.

Remember she was just released from custody, and we are now tracking, and waiting for her first court date, but we're doing more than 99.9 percent of people in her same position. She is well on her way to changing the perception of her case. She is dealing with what happened on a personal level, so when we go to court, she is far along on the path to turning this into a positive learning experience

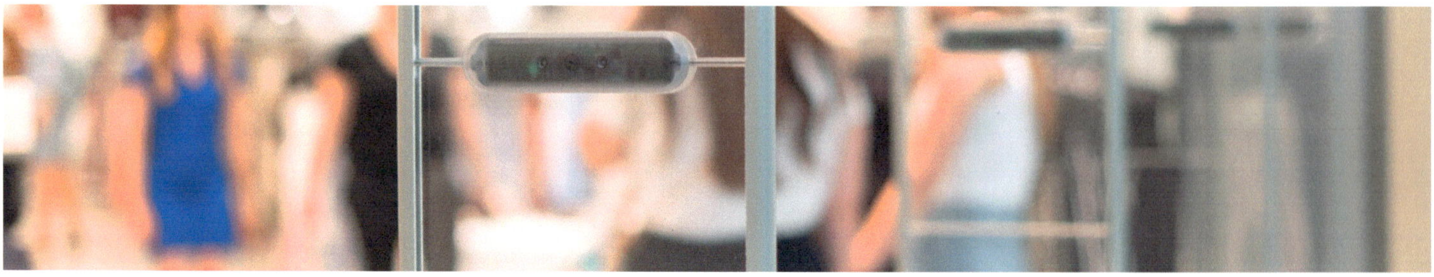

We can never be sure something will not happen again, but at least we have created a track record and some tangible evidence that she is working to make better choices. The final step in our proactive plan would be some community engagement. I tell Jennifer that I want her to do some legwork and final non-profit which she is passionate about. Her stealing from the store is a negative moment in the community.

The store workers, police, jail, prosecutor and judge have now all touched her case, because of her actions; these are public resources. We want to counteract these negative vibes with some positive steps in our same community. We certainly want to avoid the judge's wrath that Jennifer "need to learn a lesson".

By taking these four proactive steps, she has demonstrated how seriously she is taking the incident and has self-imposed a number of steps.
When we now go to court and work with the prosecutor, and judge, they are more likely to be open to creative solutions of resolution for her case.

What started off as a thief stealing from the store, and now turned into a mother of 3, having personal difficult at work and at home, which contributed to a lapse in judgment, and an isolated poor choice. If the prosecutor, and judge go along with this new theme, or "true impression" we are likely to be able to provide Jennifer a path to dismissal and keeping this off her record.

Along with a great result at the courthouse, she now has built up an alternative track record/path of redemption if she needs to further explain the incident to the licensing board, and to keep her job. She is no longer just hoping things work out, she has earned an extraordinary result.

Charged with MDOP, what can we do next?

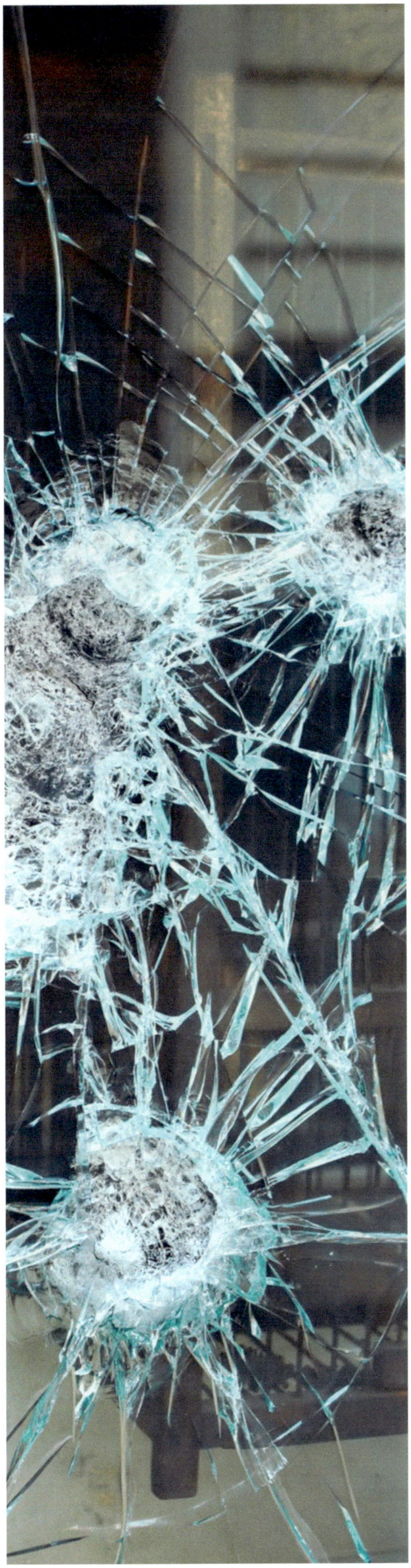

Brian reaches out to me about a recent incident involving a neighbor. Brian is a family man who has never had issues with the law but doesn't get along with his next-door neighbor.

He has two children and has been teaching at the same high school for 20 years. He loves what he does professionally but is now charged with Malicious Destruction of Property. He is worried about losing his job and having a criminal record due to an isolated poor choice.

Once Brian reaches out, I confirm his age, criminal history, his job, if he holds any licenses through the State of Michigan, such as a CPL, CDL or professional license. We then get into the details of the case.

Brian has been frustrated that his neighbor has been leaving his gardening tools on the sidewalk. Brian has tripped over these tools in the past and is worried that his kids can't safely ride their bikes with tools laying around.

When this happened in the past, he would either storm away furious, but leave the tools, or toss them back onto the neighbor's property. This last time, he was so mad to see the tools on the sidewalk that he snapped one of the tools in half and tossed them onto the neighbor's grass. He went into his home and started making dinner for his family.

About an hour later, he got a knock at the door from the local police department. The neighbor had witnessed what happened and showed the police video footage from his security camera. Confronted with this information, Brian was honest and admitted to breaking the tool, but tried to give the backstory to the police; they did not care, issued Brian a ticket and left.

So, this is quite common. A client who respects the law, works hard, is a good family man, who is law abiding and generally gets along with everybody. If you told any of Brian's friends that he was charged with a crime, they would be shocked. But this is how people get in trouble with the law.

Someone comes home after a long day, is frustrated about something, feels justified in their actions, and acts out in an irrational manner, which at the time doesn't seem like a big deal, but when they reflect back, they realize how short-sighted their decision was. The neighbor appears to be wrong doer here; he leaves out his tools on a regular basis, and "deserved what happened". Morally, maybe, but the law charges Brian.

The police did not care to hear Brian's story, and Brian is now left with his entire future in jeopardy. Here is how we approach this case in a proactive fashion.

We are dealing with facts where my client is 100 percent guilty of the offense. We likely don't have any viable defense here. He purposely destroyed someone's property without permission.

The police had no interest in the background of the case, and a prosecutor may not care either. How do we change this?

We need to take the focus off the five seconds of lapse in judgment here. Brian's future should not be determined by this flash in time. That's not equitable; nobody was injured, tools can be replaced, and Brian genuinely feels bad about what he did, and 100 percent regrets what he did. The problem we run into is "words mean very little" when we go to court.

As a former prosecutor I would review the case and know that Brian clearly broke the law, and there's punishment for that. I would also picture Brian as an angry person who does this all the time, I have no idea that he is a teacher, with a family and no prior history. The prosecutor will never go outside the four corners of the police report without Brian and his attorney being proactive.

As Brian's attorney, I recommend that he sit down and meet with a counselor. Someone who is professionally trained in mental and emotional health, who can help Brian best understand what triggered his reaction. It's important that Brian fully understand what built up to his rash choice to break the neighbor's tool.

It's also important that this third-party professional have a chance to meet Brian, and can put together a full report for our case. A report that highlights his past, present and his future plans. It carries more weight for this counselor to lay this out in an evaluation, vs me as his attorney.

To be able to say a counselor met with Brian, and here's why it happened, but also the counselor has determined that stress from work, and a continued triggering by the neighbor's behavior lead to this incident. The counselor recommends that Brian come twice per month and continue to express his feelings, and work toward better conflict resolution.

We have now made sense of the case for the prosecutor and provided the "other side". Nobody wants to hear from Brian, because it sounds like a bunch of excuses. Having an attorney go in there and say all this is hot air too, but I'm not trained to evaluate Brian's mental and emotional help and help him deal better with conflicts.

Brian is no longer a "wild card". He is no longer someone unpredictable with an assumed history of violent acts of destroying property of others. We have made his family, career and lack of past criminal history relevant, and provided context and a future plan to ensure this does not happen again.

We also realize that breaking the law should carry a punitive measure, and we certainly don't want that to be jail or 24 months of court supervision. There is no alcohol or drug use here, and we would like to avoid expensive testing.

We decide to do two days of proactive community service with a local charity as a way to give back and put positive vibes back into the community. Breaking the neighbor's property was a negative act, so we do our best to counteract that.

We of course fully agree to replace the gardening tool, even buy the neighbor a better version of the tool if he chooses. We are willing to write an apology letter and have no further contact with the neighbor if that is their desire as well.

With all of these positive vibes in the case, and our willingness to make things right, the prosecutor is now in a position to justify working with us on an extraordinary outcome.

Because all courts, prosecutors and judges are different, I don't want to get into any specific outcome, but based on what we did for Brian so far, I would be confident that the prosecutor would give us a path to potential dismissal, the ability to move forward without a criminal record, and for the judge to our proactive work without the need to impose jail, or any long-term court supervision.

We may be in a position where we continue our progress with the counselor, pay the gardening tool, and have no further incidents during a short period of time; if we achieve all of that, we have given Brian a true second chance of redemption.

Brian has learned a valuable life lesson that you need to think twice about your decisions, even if they feel justified, or you'll get away with doing it. Assume the worst could happen and learn how to deal with conflict going forward.

We have no turned Brian's case into a success. Things happen for a reason, and without this run-in with the neighbor, something worse may have happened in the future without this intervention.

Brian in the end created a manageable outcome for himself, because he was open to be being proactive, and took steps to address the underlying issues before being told to do so by a prosecutor and judge. He realized that despite the stress, anxiety and worries during this case, that he is in a better position to go forward as an educator, family man, and member of the community.

52-1 DISTRICT COURT- NOVI
OAKLAND COUNTY

JUDGE BONDY

JUDGE REEDS

JUDGE LAW

If charged with a misdemeanor in the Novi, South Lyon, Milford, Wolverine Lake or Commerce Township, the case will be heard by Judge Robert Bondy, Judge Travis Reeds or Judge David Law who handle the cases at the 52-1 District Court. The prosecutor will either be an assistant prosecutor from Oakland County Prosecutor's Office, which is lead by Jessica Cooper or one of the local prosecutors for Novi, Milford, South Lyon, Commerce Township or Wolverine Lake.

If charged with a felony, the case will begin at the District Court for potential preliminary examination. This hearing will either be held or waived; the case would then proceed to the 6th Circuit Court.

52-2 DISTRICT COURT -CLARKSTON OAKLAND COUNTY

JUDGE FABRIZIO **JUDGE KOSTIN**

If charged with a misdemeanor in the White Lake Township, Clarkston, Holly, Groveland, Independence Township, Rose Township, Ortonville or Brandon Township, the case will be heard by Judge Joseph Fabrizio or Judge Kelley Kostin who handle the cases at the 52-2 District Court. The prosecutor will either be an assistant prosecutor from Oakland County Prosecutor's Office, which is lead by Jessica Cooper or one of the local prosecutors for White Lake Township, Clarkston, Holly, Groveland, Independence Township, Rose Township, Ortonville or Brandon Township.

If charged with a felony, the case will begin at the District Court for potential preliminary examination. This hearing will either be held or waived; the case would then proceed to the 6th Circuit Court.

This court will not waive the arraignment for an attorney and client. Instead a due date will be set to "turn yourself in", which sounds scary, but with an attorney, and a proactive plan in place, it is quite straight forward and fruitful.

52-3 DISTRICT COURT- ROCHESTER HILLS
OAKLAND COUNTY

JUDGE CARNIAK

JUDGE ASADOORIAN

JUDGE NICHOLSON

If charged with a misdemeanor in the City of Rochester, Rochester Hills, Auburn Hills, Oxford, Orion Twp, Lake Orion, Addison Twp and the Village of Leonard, the case will be heard by Judge Nancy Carinak, Judge Julie Nicholson or Judge Lisa Asadoorian who handle cases at the 52-3 District Court. The prosecutor will either be an assistant prosecutor from Oakland County Prosecutor's Office, which is lead by Jessica Cooper or one of the local prosecutors for Auburn Hills, City of Rochester, Rochester Hill, Orion, Oxford etc. If charged with a felony, the case will begin at the District Court for potential preliminary examination. This hearing will either be held or waived; the case would then proceed to the 6th Circuit Court.

This court will not waive the arraignment, and will set a due date to turn yourself in with your attorney. This is not a bad thing if you're prepared and on top of your game.

Clients should be prepared to stick to a zero tolerance on hiccups and issues while on bond with the court, and expect tough recommendations from probation. The bar is set very high in this court, and we put a proactive program in place to reach those heights.

52-4 DISTRICT COURT -TROY
OAKLAND COUNTY

JUDGE HARTIG

JUDGE MCGINNIS

If charged with a misdemeanor in the City of Troy or Clawson, the case will be heard by Judge Kirsten Hartig or Judge Maureen McGinnis who handle the cases at the 52-4 District Court. The prosecutor will either be an assistant prosecutor from Oakland County Prosecutor's Office, which is lead by Jessica Cooper or the City of Clawson attorney or City of Troy Prosecutor Lori Bluhm and her assistant prosecutors.

If charged with a felony, the case will begin at the District Court for potential preliminary examination. This hearing will either be held or waived; the case would then proceed to the 6th Circuit Court.
This court will usually not waive the arraignment for an attorney and client. Instead a due date will be set to "turn yourself in", which sounds scary, but with an attorney, and a proactive plan in place, it is quite straight forward and fruitful.

This is a good court to achieve very favorable results; this will vary depending upon which prosecutor and judge is assigned to your case, and of course the facts of your case, and how well you do on my proactive program.

47TH DISTRICT COURT -FARMINGTON HILLS
OAKLAND COUNTY

JUDGE BRADY **JUDGE PARKER**

If charged with a misdemeanor in the City of Farmington or Farmington Hills the case will be heard by Judge Mark Parker or Judge James Brady who handle the cases at the 47th District Court. The prosecutor will either be an assistant prosecutor from Oakland County Prosecutor's Office, which is lead by Jessica Cooper or one of the local prosecutors for City of Farmington or Farmington Hills.

This court is good about working with attorneys about waiving arraignments and setting pretrials. We can then get proactive during this period of time. This allows us to have productive conversations with the prosecutor and judge, and push the "real you" vs the 4 corners of the police report, which don't fairly represent who my client is in the past, present and future.

If charged with a felony, the case will begin at the District Court for potential preliminary examination. This hearing will either be held or waived; the case would then proceed to the 6th Circuit Court.

44TH DISTRICT COURT -ROYAL OAK
OAKLAND COUNTY

JUDGE MEINECKE   JUDGE WITTENBERG

If charged with a misdemeanor in Royal Oak or Berkley, the case will be heard by Judge Derek Meinecke or Judge Wittenberg who handle the cases at the 44th District Court. The prosecutor will either be the City of Royal Oak or Berkley or an assistant prosecutor from Oakland County Prosecutor's Office, which is lead by Jessica Cooper.The most common police departments making arrests are the Oakland County Sheriff, Royal PD, Berkley PD and the Michigan State Police.

If charged with a felony, the case will begin at the District Court for potential preliminary examination. This hearing will either be held or waived; the case would then proceed to the 6th Circuit Court.

This court will not waive the arraignment for the attorney and client; instead an arraignment will be set to attend, and bond conditions will be put in place. The goal for my clients is to come prepared to this arraignment with a series of proactive steps already in place in order to begin to change the perception of the case on day one.

46TH DISTRICT COURT- SOUTHFIELD OAKLAND COUNTY

JUDGE NANCE

JUDGE ARVANT

JUDGE JOHNSON

If charged with a misdemeanor in Southfield, Lathrup Village, Beverly Hills, Franklin Village, Bingham Farms, the case will be heard by Judge Debra Nance, Cynthia Arvant and Sheila Johnson who handle the at the 46th District Court. The prosecutor will either be the City of Southfield, one of the other local prosecutos or an assistant prosecutor from Oakland County Prosecutor's Office, which is lead by Jessica Cooper. The most common police departments making arrests are the Oakland County Sheriff, Southfield PD and the Michigan State Police.

The 46th Court sometimes will agree to waive the arraignment, it's a bit hit or miss with the clerks and the staff. My clients will prepare for either scenario and be working on a series of proactive steps in order to make a great TRUE impression on the court, as we work away from the impression of the report.

If charged with a felony, the case will begin at the District Court for potential preliminary examination. This hearing will either be held or waived; the case would then proceed to the 6th Circuit Court.

45A DISTRICT COURT -OAK PARK
OAKLAND COUNTY

JUDGE GUBOW **JUDGE APPEL**

If charged with a misdemeanor in Huntington Woods, Oak Park, and Pleasant Ridge, the case will be heard by Judge David Gubow or Judge Michelle Friedman Appel who handle the drunk driving cases at the 45th District Court.

The prosecutor will either be the City of Oak Park, Huntington Woods or Pleasant Ridge or an assistant prosecutor from Oakland County Prosecutor's Office, which is lead by Jessica Cooper.The most common police departments making arrests are the Oakland County Sheriff, Oak Park PD and the Michigan State Police.

If charged with a felony, the case will begin at the District Court for potential preliminary examination. This hearing will either be held or waived; the case would then proceed to the 6th Circuit Court.

48TH DISTRICT COURT- BLOOMFIELD HILLS OAKLAND COUNTY

JUDGE SMALL

JUDGE D'AGOSTINI

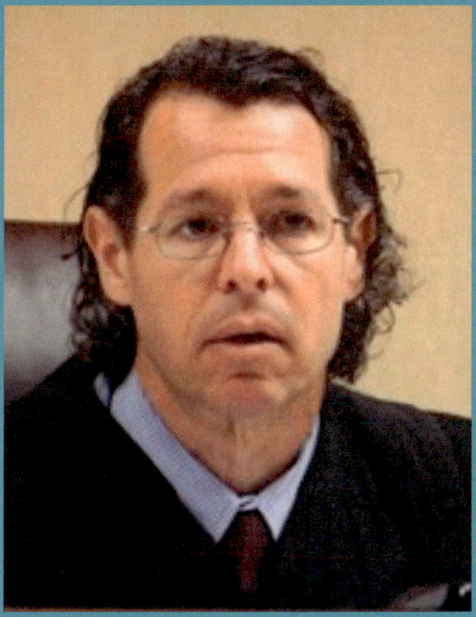

JUDGE BARRON

If charged with a misdemeanor in the Charter Township of Bloomfield, Charter Township of West Bloomfield, City of Birmingham, City of Bloomfield Hills, Keego Harbor, Orchard Lake Village and Sylvan Lake, the case will be heard by Judge Marc Barron, Judge Kimberly Small or Judge Diane D'Agostini who handle the cases at the 48th District Court. The prosecutor will either be an assistant prosecutor from Oakland County Prosecutor's Office, which is lead by Jessica Cooper or one of the following:

City of Birmingham & City of Orchard Lake Village - Mary Kucharek
City of Bloomfield Hills - Jennifer Hills
Charter Township of Bloomfield & City of Sylvan Lake - Charles D. Snell
City of Keego Harbor - Thomas J. Ryan
Charter Township of West Bloomfield - Larry Sherman

If charged with a felony, the case will begin at the District Court for potential preliminary examination. This hearing will either be held or waived; the case would then proceed to the 6th Circuit Court.

51ST DISTRICT COURT -WATERFORD OAKLAND COUNTY

JUDGE FOX **JUDGE KUHN**

If charged with a misdemeanor in Waterford Township, the case will be heard by Judge Todd Fox and Richard Kuhn Jr. who handle the cases at the 51st District Court. The prosecutor will either be the Waterford Township or an assistant prosecutor from Oakland County Prosecutor's Office, which is lead by Jessica Cooper.The most common police departments making arrests are the Oakland County Sheriff, Waterford PD and the Michigan State Police.

If charged with a felony, the case will begin at the District Court for potential preliminary examination. This hearing will either be held or waived; the case would then proceed to the 6th Circuit Court.

The Waterford court has fair prosecutors and good judges. The court will typically waive arraignments for clients and be flexible with court dates. This allows my client to build up a strong proactive resume on my program. We want to come to court prepared and ready to change the perception of the file. Without this approach, it's very easy for a defendant to become a name and a charge with no further inquiry by the judge and prosecutor.

43RD DISTRICT COURT- HAZEL PARK, FERNDALE & MADISON HEIGHTS

JUDGE LONGO

JUDGE HUNT

JUDGE GOEDERT

If you are charged with a misdemeanor offense in Ferndale, Hazel Park or Madison Heights your case will be heard at the 43rd District Court. If you are charged with a felony offense in Ferndale, Hazel Park or Madison Heights your case will begin at the 43rd District Court for preliminary examination then proceed to the Oakland County Circuit Court for trial.

The presiding judges at the 43rd District Court are the Honorable Joseph Longo, Charles G. Goedert and Keith P. Hunt.

The prosecuting attorney in Oakland County is Jessica Cooper who is the elected official in charge of the Oakland County Prosecutor's Office; each city within this jurisdiction has their own prosecutor.

The types of deals and outcomes really vary for these three courts, but the same thing holds true for every court; being proactive works!

Every one of my clients is proactive from day one as we prepare to change the perception with the judge and the various prosecutors.

50TH DISTRICT COURT- PONTIAC OAKLAND COUNTY

JUDGE GROSS

JUDGE THOMAS

JUDGE WALKER

JUDGE WALKER

If you are charged with a misdemeanor offense in Pontiac your case will be heard at the 50th District Court, which is located at 70 N. Saginaw Pontiac, MI 48342.If you are charged with a felony offense in Pontiac your case will begin at the 50th District Court for preliminary examination then proceed to the Oakland County Circuit Court for trial.

The presiding judges at the Pontiac District Court are
the Honorable Michael Martinez, Preston G. Thomas, Ronda Fowlkes Gross and Cynthia Thomas Walker. The prosecuting attorney in Oakland County is Jessica Cooper who is the elected official in charge of the Oakland County Prosecutor's Office.

16TH DISTRICT COURT- LIVONIA
WAYNE COUNTY

JUDGE MCCANN

JUDGE KAVANAGH

If charged with a misdemeanor in Livonia the case will be heard by Judge Sean Kavanagh and Judge Kathleen McCann who handle the cases at the 16th District Court. The prosecutor will either be the City of Livonia Paul Bernier or an assistant prosecutor from Wayne County, which is lead by Kim Worthy.

The most common police departments are the Wayne County Sheriff, Livonia PD and the Michigan State Police.The 16th District Court does have a sobriety court, which is a useful consideration if a client is charged with a second offense.

If charged with a felony, the case will begin at the District Court for potential preliminary examination. This hearing will either be held or waived; the case would then proceed to the 3rd Circuit Court.

17TH DISTRICT COURT- REDFORD WAYNE COUNTY

JUDGE HAROUTUNIAN

JUDGE KHALIL

If you are charged with a Michigan misdemeanor offense in Redford your case will be heard at the 17th District Court, which is located at 15111 Beech-Daly Rd Redford, MI 48239.

If you are charged with a Michigan felony offense in Redford, your case will begin at the 17th District Court for preliminary examination then proceed to the Wayne County Circuit Court for trial.The presiding judges at the Redford District Court are the Honorable Karen Khalil and the Honorable Krista Haroutunian.

The prosecuting attorney in Wayne County is Kym L. Worthy who is the elected official in charge of the Wayne County Prosecutor's Office.

18TH DISTRICT COURT- WESTLAND
WAYNE COUNTY

JUDGE CICIRELLI **JUDGE MCCONNELL**

If charged with a misdemeanor in Westland the case will be heard by Judge McConnell and Judge Cicirelli who handle the cases at the 18th District Court. The prosecutor will either be the City of Westland or an assistant prosecutor from Wayne County, which is lead by Kim Worthy.

The most common police departments are the Wayne County Sheriff, Westland PD and the Michigan State Police.

If charged with a felony, the case will begin at the District Court for potential preliminary examination. This hearing will either be held or waived; the case would then proceed to the 3rd Circuit Court.

19TH DISTRICT COURT- DEARBORN WAYNE COUNTY

JUDGE SOMERS

JUDGE HUNT

JUDGE SALAMEY

If charged with a misdemeanor in Dearborn, the case will be heard by Judge Gene Hunt, Judge Mark Somers and Judge Sam Salamey who handle the cases at the 19th District Court. The prosecutor will either be the City of Dearborn or an assistant prosecutor from Wayne County, which is lead by Kim Worthy.

The most common police departments are the Wayne County Sheriff, Dearborn Heights PD and the Michigan State Police. Most first offenses at this court are handled by the City of Dearborn, but all repeat offenders will be charged by the County.

If charged with a felony, the case will begin at the District Court for potential preliminary examination. This hearing will either be held or waived; the case would then proceed to the 3rd Circuit Court.

20TH DISTRICT COURT- DEARBORN HEIGHTS
WAYNE COUNTY

JUDGE PLAWECKI

JUDGE TURFE

If charged with a misdemeanor in Dearborn Heights the case will be heard by Judge David Turfe and Judge Plawecki who handle the cases at the 20th District Court. The prosecutor will either be the City of Dearborn Heights or an assistant prosecutor from Wayne County, which is lead by Kim Worthy.

The most common police departments are the Wayne County Sheriff, Dearborn Heights PD and the Michigan State Police. This court generally waives the walk-in arraignment and will cancel any warrant on a first offense drunk driving case.

If charged with a felony, the case will begin at the District Court for potential preliminary examination. This hearing will either be held or waived; the case would then proceed to the 3rd Circuit Court.

23RD DISTRICT COURT- TAYLOR
WAYNE COUNTY

JUDGE SALOMONE & SLAVEN

If charged with a misdemeanor in Taylor, the case will be heard by Judge Geno D. Salomone and Judge Joseph D. Slaven who handle the cases at the 23rd District Court. The prosecutor will either be the City of Taylor or an assistant prosecutor from Wayne County, which is lead by Kim Worthy.

The most common police departments are the Wayne County Sheriff, Taylor PD and the Michigan State Police. This court generally waives the walk-in arraignment and will cancel any warrant on a first offense drunk driving case.

If charged with a felony, the case will begin at the District Court for potential preliminary examination. This hearing will either be held or waived; the case would then proceed to the 3rd Circuit Court.

24TH DISTRICT COURT- ALLEN PARK
WAYNE COUNTY

JUDGE COURTWRIGHT

JUDGE PAGE

If you're charged with a misdemeanor offense in Allen Park your case will be heard at the 24th District Court, which is located at 6515 Roosevelt Rd.Allen Park, MI 48101.

If you are charged with a felony offense in Allen Park, your case will begin at the 24th District Court for preliminary examination then proceed to the Wayne County Circuit Court for trial.

The presiding judges at the Allen Park District Court are the Honorable John T. Courtright and Honorable Richard A. Page. The prosecuting attorney in Wayne County is Kym L. Worthy who is the elected official in charge of the Wayne County Prosecutor's Office.

21TH DISTRICT COURT- GARDEN CITY
WAYNE COUNTY

JUDGE HAMMER

If charged with a misdemeanor in Garden City, the case will be heard by Judge Richard Hammer who handles the cases at the 21st District Court. The prosecutor will either be the City of Garden City or an assistant prosecutor from Wayne County, which is lead by Kim Worthy.

The most common police departments are the Wayne County Sheriff, Garden City PD and the Michigan State Police. This court generally waives the walk-in arraignment and will cancel any warrant on a first offense drunk driving case.

If charged with a felony, the case will begin at the District Court for potential preliminary examination. This hearing will either be held or waived; the case would then proceed to the 3rd Circuit Court.

25TH DISTRICT COURT- LINCOLN PARK, ECORSE & RIVER ROUGE WAYNE COUNTY

JUDGE ZELENAK & CLIFTON

If you are charged with a Michigan misdemeanor offense in Lincoln Park or River Rouge your case will be heard at the 25th District Court, which is located at 1475 Cleophus Lincoln Park, MI 48146.If you are charged with a Michigan felony offense in Lincoln Park, your case will begin at the 25th District Court for preliminary examination then proceed to the Wayne County Circuit Court for trial.

The presiding judges at the Lincoln Park District Court are the Honorable David J. Zelenak & Gregory Clifton.

The prosecuting attorney in Wayne County is Kym L. Worthy who is the elected official in charge of the Wayne County Prosecutor's Office.

27TH DISTRICT COURT- WYANDOTTE & RIVERVIEW - WAYNE COUNTY

JUDGE ELIZABETH L. DISANTO

If charged with a misdemeanor in the Wyandotte or Riverview, the case will be heard by Judge Elizabeth Disanto who handles the cases at the 27th District Court.

The prosecutor will either be one of the local prosecutors for Riverview or Wyandotte or an assistant prosecutor from Wayne County, which is lead by Kim Worthy. The most common police departments are the Wayne County Sheriff, Wyandotte PD, Riverview PD and the Michigan State Police.

If charged with a felony, the case will begin at the District Court for potential preliminary examination. This hearing will either be held or waived; the case would then proceed to the 3rd Circuit Court.

28TH DISTRICT COURT- SOUTHGATE

JUDGE JAMES KANDREVAS

If you are charged with a Michigan misdemeanor offense in Southgate your case will be heard at the 28th District Court, which is located at 14720 Reaume Parkway Southgate, MI 48195.

If you are charged with a Michigan felony offense in Southgate, your case will begin at the 28th District Court for preliminary examination then proceed to the Wayne County Circuit Court for trial.The presiding judges at the Southgate District Court is the Honorable James A. Kandrevas.

The prosecuting attorney in Wayne County is Kym L. Worthy who is the elected official in charge of the Wayne County Prosecutor's Office. I've found Judge Kandrevas to be very fair and open to my client's proactive efforts prior to going to court. He has shown both an understanding appreciation for my clients stepping up and getting themselves on the right path.

30TH DISTRICT COURT - HIGHLAND
31ST DISTRICT COURT - HAMTRAMCK
32A - HARPER WOODS

12050 Woodward Ave.
Highland Park, MI 48203
(313) 252-0300
Honorable Brigette Officer Holley, Chief Judge

3401 Evaline Ave.
Hamtramck, MI 48212
(313) 800-5248
Honorable Alexis G. Krot, Chief Judge

19617 Harper Ave.
Harper Woods, MI 48225(313) 343-2590
Honorable Daniel S. Palmer, Chief Judge

I've grouped these three courts together because they are smaller courts that don't see any cases at other courts. This means that when a client comes well prepared, organized, and on top of their case, they can really stand out. My clients are proactive from day one, and have blown these judges and courts out of the water with how they changed the perception of their case on day one.

These courts tend to have less probation support and not as many resources, which means my clients have a good chance of demonstrating that they can make good choices and stay on track with or without the court telling them what to do. I've had numerous clients receive no probation, because of our game plan for the case.

36TH DISTRICT COURT
WAYNE COUNTY

Frank Murphy Hall of Justice
1441 St. Antoine
Detroit, MI 48226
(313) 224-2506

Honorable William C. McConico, Chief Judge
Honorable Lydia Nance Adams, District Judge
Honorable Roberta C. Archer, District Judge
Honorable Christopher Michael Blount, District Judge
Honorable Nancy McCaughan Blount, District Judge
Honorable Demetria Brue, District Judge
Honorable Esther Lynise Bryant, District Judge
Honorable Donald Coleman, District Judge
Honorable Kahlilia Yvette Davis, District Judge
Honorable Deborah Geraldine Ford, District Judge
Honorable Austin William Garrett, District Judge
Honorable Kristina Robinson Garrett, District Judge
Honorable Ruth Ann Garrett, District Judge
Honorable Ronald Giles, District Judge
Honorable Adrienne Hinnant-Johnson, District Judge
Honorable Shannon A. Holmes, District Judge
Honorable Patricia L. Jefferson, District Judge
Honorable Kenyetta Stanford Jones, District Judge
Honorable Alicia A. Jones-Coleman, District Judge
Honorable Kenneth J. King, District Judge
Honorable Deborah L. Langston, District Judge
Honorable Jacquelyn A. McClinton, District Judge
Honorable Donna R. Milhouse, District Judge
Honorable B. Pennie Millender, District Judge
Honorable Kevin F. Robbins, District Judge
Honorable David S. Robinson, Jr., District Judge
Honorable Aliyah Sabree, District Judge
Honorable Michael E. Wagner, District Judge
Honorable Larry D. Williams, Jr., District Judge

The 36th District Court is extremely busy and overworked. It is not always easy to get the proper attention for a client who has put in the proactive hard work on day one, but it is very possible. Be prepared to work extra hard to change the perception of your case in Downtown Detroit.

GROSSE POINTE COURTS

City of Grosse Pointe
17147 Maumee
Grosse Pointe, MI 48230
(313) 343-5262
Honorable Russell F. Ethridge, Chief Judge

Grosse Pointe Park
15115 E. Jefferson Ave.
Grosse Pte. Park, MI 48230
(313) 822-3535
Honorable Carl F. Jarboe, Chief Judge

Grosse Pointe Woods
20025 Mack Plaza Drive
Grosse Pte. Woods, MI 48236
(313) 343-2455
Honorable Theodore A. Metry, Chief Judge

The Grosse Point courts are Munipical Courts that have judges who also practice law as private attorneys. It is a small-town feel to every case, but both prosecutors and judges have been very receptive to my client's proactive steps. With smaller caseloads, it's a bit easier to stand out among a smaller crowd.

Clients should expect to be treated fairly, and offered a chance of redemption, but extraordinary results must be earned, not handed out.

33RD DISTRICT COURT- WOODHAVEN
WAYNE COUNTY

Scouting Report

If charged with a misdemeanor in the Townships of Brownstown and Grosse Ile, and the Cities of Flat Rock, Gibraltar, Rockwood, Trenton, and Woodhaven the case will be heard by Judge McNally, Hesson or Kersten who handle the cases at the 33rd District Court. The prosecutor will either be one of the local prosecutors for Woodhaven, Brownstown, Flat Rock, Trenton or an assistant prosecutor from Wayne County, which is lead by Kim Worthy.

The most common police departments are the Wayne County Sheriff, Woodhaven PD, Brownstown Township, Flat Rock, Trenton and the Michigan State Police.

If charged with a felony, the case will begin at the District Court for potential preliminary examination. This hearing will either be held or waived; the case would then proceed to the 3rd Circuit Court.

35TH DISTRICT COURT- PLYMOUTH, NORTHVILLE & CANTON WAYNE COUNTY

JUDGE LOWE JUDGE GEROU JUDGE PLAKAS

If charged with a misdemeanor in Plymouth, Canton or Northville the case will be heard by Judge Lowe, Gerou or Plakas who handle the cases at the 35th District Court. The prosecutor will either be one of the local prosecutors for Northville Township, City of Northville, Canton, Canton Township, Plymouth or Plymouth Township or an assistant prosecutor from Wayne County, which is lead by Kim Worthy.

The most common police departments are the Wayne County Sheriff, Canton Township, Plymouth, Northville Township, City of Northville and the Michigan State Police.

I've been able to work out great outcomes for my clients who are willing to be proactive from day one. The judges and prosecutors at the 35th court are open to giving second chances to clients to demonstrate the right approach and mindset. If charged with a felony, the case will begin at the District Court for potential preliminary examination. This hearing will either be held or waived; the case would then proceed to the 3rd Circuit Court.

34TH DISTRICT COURT- ROMULUS
WAYNE COUNTY

JUDGE GREEN JUDGE OAKLEY JUDGE PARROT

If charged with a misdemeanor DUI in Romulus, New Boston, Huron Township, Belleville, Van Buren Township, Detroit Metro Airport or Sumpter Township the case will be heard by Judge Parrot, Green or Oakley who handle the drunk driving cases at the 34th District Court.

The prosecutor will either be one of the local prosecutors for Romulus, Belleville, Van Buren Township, the special airport prosecutor or an assistant prosecutor from Wayne County, which is lead by Kim Worthy. The most common police departments are the Wayne County Sheriff, Romulus PD, Huron Twp PD, Belleville, Van Buren Township, Detroit Metro Airport, Sumpter Township and the Michigan State Police.

The Romulus court is a very receptive court to proactive clients. This court also has a sobriety court, which may be useful for a repeat offender. I've found all of the prosecutor's and judges to be very fair, reasonable and open-minded about proactive efforts prior to my client appearing in court. The results have reflected the work.

15TH DISTRICT COURT- ANN ARBOR WASHTENAW COUNTY

JUDGE HINES

JUDGE VALVO

JUDGE BURKE

The 15th District Court in Ann Arbor is very fair and reasonable court for misdemeanor cases. All three judges are fair to both sides, and the two prosecutor's are open to second chances. Judge Hines and Valvo handle all criminal cases, and the City of Ann Arbor and Washtenaw County are the prosecutors.

The 15th District Court will generally allow an attorney to help a client avoid a warrant for arrest, and set an Arraignment/Pretrial date with the court. At this hearing, bond conditions such as alcohol testing may be imposed, but we prepare for this by putting testing in place on our own. Client's should expect the opportunity to be proactive, and for the hard work to payoff. Both judges are very accommodating and willing to support a client's journey in changing the perception of their case.

If charged with a felony, the case will begin at the District Court for potential preliminary examination. This hearing will either be held or waived; the case would then proceed to the 22nd Circuit Court.

Cases at the 15th District Court generally last between 45 and 120 days from beginning to cend result for the client. If the case goes to trial, the timeline may be extended.

14A DISTRICT COURT- ANN ARBOR
WASHTENAW COUNTY

JUDGE TABBEY JUDGE SIMPSON JUDGE FRUSHOUR

The 14A District Court in Washtenaw County has four locations (Saline, Ypsilanti, Pittsfield & Chelsea). All three judges handle criminal cases; clients can really advance their case and earn the benefit of the doubt by being proactive.

I've had clients earn dismissals, reductions, and very favorable sentences, such as mo probation or jail, because of our efforts. All four courts are reasonable and flexible when it comes to setting court dates vs issuing arrest warrants. Depending on which judge is on your case, you may be ordered to wear an alcohol tether, or an alternative testing option can be arranged. My clients come to court already as we want to create the most favorable environment with the judge and prosecutor.

If charged with a felony, the case will begin at the District Court for potential preliminary examination. This hearing will either be held or waived; the case would then proceed to the 6th Circuit Court.

Washtenaw County is the main prosecutor, but City of Ypsilanti, Pittsfield Township. City of Saline, Milan, EMU, Superior Township and other jurisdictions have their own prosecuting attorney.

14B DISTRICT COURT- ANN ARBOR
WASHTENAW COUNTY

JUDGE POPE

Scouting Report

The 14B Court is located in Ypsilanti Township, and is its own branch of the 14th District Court. Judge Pope is the current judge, but is soon retirning from his years of service. The magistrate is Mark Nelson, who is also running to be the new judge.

This court will allow an attorney to avoid an arrest warrant for a client, and set a case for an arraignment/pretrial. This allows my clients extra time to be proactive, and come to court as prepared as possible in order to change the perception of their case with the judge and prosecutor.

The court has two prosecutors; Washtenaw County and Ypsilanti Township. Cases are generally assigned by the police department that makes the arrest, but all felonies would be prosecuted by the County.

Judge Pope is very fair and reasonable if a client comes prepared to court. All of my clients take proactive steps to put our best foot forward with the prosecutor and the judge. My clients have also had excellent experiences with the probation department. This court has a speciality court, which acts as a sobriety court for the right client.

MACOMB COUNTY

All misdemeanor cases in Macomb County will begin at the District Court level. If charged with a felony, the case may or may not proceed to the 16th Circuit Court. The first set of judges are the District Court judges, The next set are the Circuit Court judges.

- Clinton Township - Judge Fuca, Judge Davis & Judge Lucido
- Eastpointe- - Judge Gerds III
- Roseville & Fraser- Judge Santia, Judge Boedeker & Judge Steenland
- Shelby Township - Judge Shepherd
- Sterling Heights - Judge Sierawski, Judge Maceroni & Judge Wiegand
- St Clair Shores - Judge Fratarcangeli & Judge Oster
- New Baltimore/Romeo - Judge Biernat & Judge LeDuc
- Warren & Centerline - Judge Chmura, Judge Michael Chupa, Judge Suzanne Faunce & Judge Sabaugh

Honorable James M. Biernat, Jr., Chief Judge
Honorable Richard L. Caretti, Circuit Judge
Honorable Diane M. Druzinski, Circuit Judge
Honorable Jennifer Faunce, Circuit Judge
Honorable Julie Gatti, Circuit Judge
Honorable James M. Maceroni, Circuit Judge
Honorable Carl J. Marlinga, Circuit Judge
Honorable Rachel Rancilio, Circuit Judge
Honorable Edward A. Servitto, Jr., Circuit Judge
Honorable Michael E. Servitto, Circuit Judge
Honorable Mark S. Switalski, Circuit Judge
Honorable Matthew S. Switalski, Circuit Judge
Honorable Joseph Toia, Circuit Judge
Honorable Kathryn A. Viviano, Circuit Judge
Honorable Tracey A. Yokich, Circuit Judge

LIVINGSTON COUNTY - 53RD DISTRICT COURT & 44TH CIRCUIT COURT

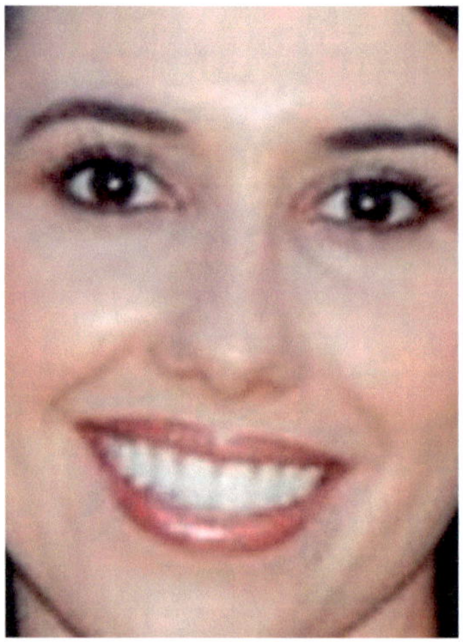

All misdemeanor cases in Livingston County will begin at the 53rd District Court level. If charged with a felony, the case may or may not proceed to the 44th Circuit Court. The District Court judges are pictured above (Daniel Bain & Shauna Murphy), the Circuit Court judges are listed below.

Honorable Michael P. Hatty, Chief Judge

Honorable L. Suzanne Geddis, Circuit Judge

Honorable Matthew J. McGivney, Circuit Judge

MONROE COUNTY - 1ST DISTRICT COURT & 38TH CIRCUIT COURT

All misdemeanor cases in Monroe County will begin at the 1st District Court level. If charged with a felony, the case may or may not proceed to the 38th Circuit Court. The District Court judges are pictured above (Jack Vitale, Michael Brown & William Nichols), the Circuit Court judges are listed below.

Honorable Michael A. Weipert, Chief Judge

Honorable Mark S. Braunlich, Circuit Judge

Honorable Daniel S. White, Circuit Judge

LENAWEE COUNTY 2A DISTRICT COURT & 39TH CIRCUIT COURT

All misdemeanor cases in Lenawee County will begin at the 2A District Court level. If charged with a felony, the case may or may not proceed to the 39th Circuit Court. The District Court judges are pictured above (Laura Schaedler & Jonathan Poer), the Circuit Court judges are listed below.

Honorable Anna Marie Anzalone, Chief Judge

Honorable Michael R. Olsaver, Circuit Judge

JACKSON COUNTY 12TH DISTRICT COURT & 4TH CIRCUIT COURT

All misdemeanor cases in Jackson County will begin at the 12th District Court level. If charged with a felony, the case may or may not proceed to the 4th Circuit Court. The District Court judges are pictured above (Judge Mazur, Klaeren, Filip and Goostrey), the Circuit Court judges are listed below.

Honorable Susan Beebe Jordan, Chief Judge
Honorable Richard N. LaFlamme, Circuit Judge
Honorable John G. McBain, Jr., Circuit Judge
Honorable Thomas D. Wilson, Circuit Judge

GENESEE COUNTY

7th Circuit Court (C07)
Serving Genesee County
Genesee County Courthouse

900 S. Saginaw St.
Flint, MI 48502
(810) 424-4355

Honorable Duncan M. Beagle, Chief Judge
Honorable Celeste D. Bell, Circuit Judge
Honorable Joseph J. Farah, Circuit Judge
Honorable John A. Gadola, Circuit Judge
Honorable Elizabeth Anne Kelly, Circuit Judge
Honorable Mark W. Latchana, Circuit Judge
Honorable David J. Newblatt, Circuit Judge
Honorable Brian S. Pickell, Circuit Judge
Honorable Michael J. Theile, Circuit Judge

District courts located in : Flint, Grand Blanc, Mount Morris and Burton

Honorable Christopher R. Odette,
Honorable William H. Crawford, II,
Honorable G. David Guinn,
Honorable Herman Marable, Jr.,
Honorable Nathaniel C. Perry, III
Honorable Mark C. McCabe
Honorable Jennifer J. Manley
Honorable Vikki Bayeh Haley
Honorable Jessica J. Hammon

INGHAM COUNTY

30th Circuit Court
Serving Ingham County
Ingham County Courthouse

PO Box 40771
Veterans Memorial Courthouse
313 W. Kalamazoo St.
Lansing, MI 48901

Honorable Richard J. Garcia, Chief Judge
Honorable Rosemarie E. Aquilina, Circuit Judge
Honorable Clinton Canady, III, Circuit Judge
Honorable Joyce Draganchuk, Circuit Judge
Honorable James S. Jamo, Circuit Judge
Honorable Janelle A. Lawless, Circuit Judge
Honorable Lisa K. McCormick, Circuit Judge

District courts located in : Lansing, East Lansing, Mason &

Honorable Louise Alderson, Chief Judge
Honorable Stacia J. Buchanan, District Judge
Honorable Kristen D. Simmons, District Judge
Honorable Cynthia M. Ward, District Judge
Honorable Andrea Andrews Larkin, Chief Judge
Honorable Richard D. Ball, District Judge
Honorable Donald L. Allen, Chief Judge
Honorable Richard L. Hillman, District Judge

OTHER COURTS

1st Circuit Court (C01)
Serving Hillsdale County
Courthouse

29 N. Howell
Hillsdale, MI 49242
(517) 437-4321

Honorable Sara S. Lisznyai, Chief Judge
Honorable Michael R. Smith, Circuit Judge

2B District Court (D02B)
Serving Hillsdale County
49 N. Howell

Hillsdale, MI 49242
(517) 437-7329

Honorable Sara S. Lisznyai, Chief Judge

OTHER COURTS

40th Circuit Court (C40)
Serving Lapeer County
Lapeer County Complex

255 Clay Street
Lapeer, MI 48446
(810) 667-0320

Honorable Nick O. Holowka, Chief Judge
Honorable Byron J. Konschuh, Circuit Judge

71A District Court (D71A)
Serving Lapeer County
Lapeer County Complex Building

255 Clay Street
Lapeer, MI 48446
(810) 667-0314

Honorable Nick O. Holowka, Chief Judge
Honorable Laura Cheger Barnard, District Judge

OTHER COURTS

31st Circuit Court (C31)
Serving St. Clair County
County Building

201 McMorran Blvd.
Port Huron, MI 48060
&
2088 South Parker
Marine City, MI 48039

Honorable Daniel J. Kelly, Chief Judge
Honorable Cynthia A. Lane, Circuit Judge
Honorable Michael L. West, Circuit Judge

72nd District Court (D72)
Serving St. Clair County
201 McMorran Blvd.

Port Huron, MI 48060
(810) 985-2072

Honorable Daniel J. Kelly, Chief Judge
Honorable Mona S. Armstrong, District Judge
Honorable Michael L. Hulewicz, District Judge
Honorable John D. Monaghan, District Judge

OTHER COURTS

57th Circuit Court (C57)
Serving Emmet County
Emmet County Building

200 Division
Petoskey, MI 49770

(231) 348-1748

Honorable Charles W. Johnson, Chief Judge

90th District Court - Emmet (D90~2)
Serving Emmet County
Emmet County, City-County Bldg.

200 Division Street
Petoskey, MI 49770
(231) 348-1750

Honorable Valerie K. Snyder, Chief Judge
Honorable Angela Lasher, District Judge

OTHER COURTS

33rd Circuit Court (C33)
Serving Charlevoix County
Charlevoix County Building

301 State Street
Charlevoix, MI 49720
(231) 547-7243

Honorable Roy C. Hayes, III, Chief Judge

90th District Court - Charlevoix (D90~1)
Serving Charlevoix County
Charlevoix County Building

301 State St.
Charlevoix, MI 49720
(231) 547-7227

Honorable Valerie K. Snyder, Chief Judge

Honorable Angela Lasher, District Judge

OTHER COURTS

13th Circuit Court - Grand Traverse (C13~2)
Serving Grand Traverse County
Grand Traverse County Courthouse

328 Washington St.
Traverse City, MI 49684
(231) 922-4701

Honorable Kevin A. Elsenheimer, Chief Judge
Honorable Thomas G. Power, Circuit Judge

86th District Court - Grand Traverse (D86~2)
Serving Grand Traverse County
Robert P. Griffin Hall of Justice

280 Washington St.
Traverse City, MI 49684
(231) 922-4580

Honorable Michael S. Stepka, Chief Judge
Honorable Robert A. Cooney, District Judge

OTHER COURTS

13th Circuit Court - Leelanau (C13~3)
Serving Leelanau County
8527 E. Government Center Dr.
Suttons Bay, MI 49682
(231) 256-9803

Honorable Kevin A. Elsenheimer, Chief Judge
Honorable Thomas G. Power, Circuit Judge

86th District Court - Leelanau (D86~3)
Serving Leelanau County

8527 E. Government Center Dr.
Suttons Bay, MI 49682
(231) 256-8250

Honorable Michael S. Stepka, Chief Judge
Honorable Robert A. Cooney, District Judge

Made in the USA
Las Vegas, NV
03 November 2026

57274966R00069